Look at what other

TurnKey Investing with Lease-Options!

Stephanie Frank
The Accidental Millionaire
Chandler, AZ
StephanieFrank.com

WOW! Matthew hits the mark with this well-laid out real estate investing strategy using lease-options. If you are an investor looking for a no-hassle, tested and profitable approach to building your real estate wealth, then get *TurnKey Investing with Lease-Options*!

In his newest book, *TurnKey Investing with Lease-Options*, Matthew Chan gives us a specific road map to personal freedom. Matthew shows the reader how the Lease-Options strategy can provide us with financial security. From how to get started and choosing an investment property, to financing and using contracts, to dealing with problem tenants and more, *TurnKey Investing with Lease-Options* tackles the tough questions and gives us the answers.

Matthew has presented everything you need to know to get started in the Lease-Options business. The book truly lives up to its name by providing simple but detailed explanations of the terms, language, and philosophy of this exciting niche of real estate investing. To put it another way, don't buy investment houses without this book!

Bob Stovall
Orange Funding Group
Danville, KY
Orangefunding.com

Troy Arment
President
Creative Home
Solutions, Inc.
Wichita, KS
ez2ownhome.com

If you are serious about investing in single-family homes, *TurnKey Investing with Lease-Options* is a must read book! Matthew explains in detail the how's and why's of his successful investing style. I know from my own investing experience that he is giving you great information not based on theory, but based on many years of being in the trenches and growing a sound real estate investment portfolio.

After reading his newest book, *TurnKey Investing with Lease-Options*, my thoughts about Matthew Chan were once again confirmed. He is a person that openly and unselfishly shares what he has mastered with others. This book gets right to the point. It is detailed and strategic, yet Matthew has presented it in a way that is comprehensive and easy to read.

As a real estate investor, I believe *Turnkey Investing with Lease-Options* is a must read for anyone considering investing in real estate. There are too many real estate books out there that do not tell the true story. Matthew shares with us the details and strategies he personally uses to successfully acquire and manage real estate.

I also highly recommend *TurnKey Investing with Lease-Options* to people who already own real estate investments. His ideas and strategies are real, and can open doors to new investment opportunities that may have not been considered or once did not seem available.

Darla Anderson
President
DAPA Inc.

TurnKey Investing with Lease-Options is a well written real estate investment book that gives a comprehensive look at how to use Lease-Options as a management strategy.

It is perfect for new investors to carry with them as a reference manual or for the more seasoned investor as refresher material. I highly recommend reading *TurnKey Investing with Lease-Options*.

Hal Hubbard
President
New Concepts, Inc.
Gilbert, AZ

TurnKey Investing with Lease-Options is an excellent resource for both beginning and experienced real estate investors. The book is written for the "real world". I appreciated that setbacks and challenges are candidly discussed. Many authors just gloss over these facts. Matthew goes through the entire process and has valuable insights on many overlooked areas.

As an experienced investor, I found several valuable "nuggets" within the book. Matthew does an excellent job describing the positioning of the property as "owner-financing" versus "rent-to-own" (I'm rewriting several of my ads). I also learned a great deal from the marketing section and how he uses his business name and the market specialization to his advantage.

TurnKey Investing with Lease-Options provides practical advice that work in the Real World!

Steve Copper
President
Golden Bear
Management, Inc
Littleton, CO

Jack Williams
Entrepreneur/
Investor
Sydney, Australia

After reading *TurnKey Investing with Lease-Options*, all I can say is WOW! This has to be the best hands-on, real life book on investing I have ever read. The book is simply fantastic to say the least. This book will undoubtedly become required reading for anyone wanting to become a professional real estate investor seeking cash flow.

Investors! Stop renting out and start lease-optioning! In *TurnKey Investing with Lease-Options*, Matthew Chan has given us a complete “soup to nuts”, easy-to-understand blueprint for turning your single family home rental business into a Lease-Option Money Machine.

Matthew literally walks you through the steps of how to find, market, and make huge profits in the little known niche of leasing with an option to buy. Turn your tenants into occupants. Evictions made easy. Let the tenant improve the value of your property while YOU reap the rewards of tax benefits, back-end profits, and appreciation. Get cash upfront from your tenant-buyer. Automate your systems and paperwork. It’s all here. I wish I had this book when I started investing in real estate.

Dean Edelson
President
Elysium Investment
Group
Sedona, AZ

Other books by Matthew S. Chan

The Intrepid Way

How to Create the Freedom You Need to Live the Life You Want!

TurnKey Investing with Lease-Options

How to Simply & Safely Create 12% Returns with Investment Property!

The Intrepid Way II – Transformation

The Secrets You Must Learn to Create Freedom in Your Life!

www.turnkeyinvesting.com

TurnKey Investing *with* Lease-Options

How to Simply & Safely Create 12% Returns with Investment Property!

Matthew S. Chan

With Contributions by Wes Weaver

Ascend Beyond Publishing
Columbus, Georgia

TurnKey Investing with Lease-Options

How to Simply & Safely Create 12% Returns with Investment Property!

Published by: Ascend Beyond Publishing
5435 Woodruff Farm Rd., #B-300
PMB 158
Columbus, GA 31907

www.ascendbeyond.com

ISBN: 0-9713947-8-4

Printed in the United States of America. First Edition.

First Printing: November 2004

Dedication

To the people who have entrusted me ...

To the people who invested with me ...

To the people who refuse to be financial victims ...

To the people who know there is a better way ...

To the people with independent mind and spirit ...

To the people who want to finish the race as a team ...

I commit this book to them. Salute.

Matthew S. Chan

This publication is designed to provide competent and reliable information in regard to the subject matter covered. It is sold with the understanding that the author and publisher are not engaged in rendering legal, accounting or other professional advice. Laws and practices often vary from state to state and country to country. If legal advice or other expert assistance is required, the services of a competent professional should be sought. The author and publisher specifically disclaim any liability that is incurred from the use or application of the contents of this book.

Table of Contents

3 How to Research the Market

4 Purchasing Investment Properties

5 Preparing the Property

6 Marketing Properties

7 Finding the Right Tenants

8 Closing the Lease-Option Transaction

9 Dealing with Defaults & Non-Payments

10 Administration

11 The TurnKey Investing Philosophy

Appendix

Introduction

In April 2000, the Technology Stocks Crash of 2000 began a three-year decline that erased trillions of dollars of investor wealth leaving dead companies and crushed retirement accounts in its wake.

As a result, the U.S. economy plummeted with the steepest decline in recent memory. Millions of jobs were lost. Unemployment climbed. Bankruptcies and foreclosures escalated. Investment and retirement accounts were decimated.

Out of all this, I am both happy and relieved to say that I was not one of these unfortunate victims.

In January 2000, I converted all my mutual fund holdings into a cash position. When the crash occurred three months later, I knew I had made the right decision to liquidate.

While some people may simply say I was lucky, there were clear indications that a crash would occur in the near future. The problem was I did not have a crystal ball to tell me exactly when it would happen. Nevertheless I escaped unscathed.

How did I manage to escape?

The Escape

In late 1999, I experienced an unusual decline in my mutual funds portfolio. While it was not the first decline I experienced that year, it was unusual because I began to realize that my allegedly stable mutual fund portfolio was becoming more volatile with each passing month.

And since the volatility of mutual funds went against everything I was taught about how mutual funds worked the previous 15 years, it seemed to me something was wrong. Very wrong. So I decided to do the only thing I knew how to do at the time. Liquidate and escape from the stock market so I could re-evaluate future investment plans.

The Change

With no expertise or experience in the stock market, I turned my investing activities to another direction. I chose to invest in small houses to produce cash flow. While many so-called investors like to buy and fix-up houses for resale, it is not what I consider true investing. That business is called property renovation. It is what many car dealers do. They buy old cars, fix them up, and resell them. They make money but it isn't investing. It is a job. The pay stops with that one transaction.

I was looking for ongoing, spendable cash flow I could count on month in, month out until I grew old. I knew once I built up a portfolio of investment property, I could stop acquiring properties at any time and not sacrifice ongoing income.

In 1999, I bought a couple of small investment houses. Although I had dealt with family rental property and rental contracts as a teenager, I was still relatively inexperienced. It is a very different experience to buy and manage your own investment property.

The Move

After a slow start and a big move to the smaller city of Columbus, Georgia, I began to quickly learn the art and science of creating a profitable system of investing that worked in my new home city. I learned through a combination of research, teachers, investor friends, seminars, courses, books, and, yes, hard-core *field experience.*

With each property I acquired and every tenant I placed, I got better at the real estate investing and management process. After a few months living in Columbus, Georgia and making a few more acquisitions, I met someone who first became my apprentice, then my friend, and eventually my business and management partner. His name is Wes Weaver. I am proud to have him as the Lead Contributor of this book.

The Growth

Since our alliance, Wes and I have gone on to acquire and manage three dozen properties for cash flow using our turnkey lease-option system.

In layman terms, we buy small investment houses and resell them with "owner-financing". *(Lease-options are generally recognized as a form of owner-financing).* We collect a small "down payment" and receive ongoing monthly payments from our tenants. We have no ongoing maintenance or repair expenses. We do very little fix up of properties, if any. And if these tenants stop paying, we have them removed and then repeat the selling process with minimal expense and effort.

We have developed our own "recipe", our own "cookie-cutter" investment system, which we call TurnKey Investing. More specifically, we do **TurnKey Investing with Lease-Options**.

The How-To Guide

Quite frankly, the information contained in this book is not a gold-mine, but a platinum-mine of information. To date, there is no book quite like this one with all the details and inside secrets we share. Some of the hard-to-find information we provide in this book came at a cost of years of experience and thousands of dollars. This book is easily worth 100 times the cover price.

Wes and I generate several thousands of dollars of spendable income each month for ourselves and our investment partners. We are proud of this fact. Our investment partners often do not have the time, expertise, or inclination to do it themselves. You will see later in the book, how we make money from buying these small investment houses and lease-optioning them out.

This book was written for a variety of reasons:

- Because of our lead position in our market niche and the number of investment properties we manage for others, more and more people we know have become interested in learning what we do, and more importantly, how we do it.

- Because we invite investment partners to work with us, this book allows us to more completely and efficiently communicate what we do without all the fluff of a brochure.

- As our management team grows, this book serves as both an instructional and operational guide into what and how we do things. It is a more concise alternative to a full-scale Operations Manual.

- For those people who choose to manage their own real estate investment portfolios, this book will be an invaluable guide to implementing the lease-option strategy in their own markets.

The Reminder

As you read this book, please keep in mind our system constantly changes and evolves as we adapt to new circumstances and situations. We reserve the right to change, update, and revise the information in this book. So keep what you read in the proper perspective.

As a bonus, I have provided a list of questions you should answer for each chapter to get the maximum benefit from this book. Remember, there will be a test. I check financial statements.

In many ways, this book was both an ambitious and challenging project. I look forward to hearing your comments, questions, and feedback. So make sure you write them down.

Until we meet, I thank you for reading this book.

Matthew S. Chan

1 The Beauty of Lease-Options

The Benefits of Lease-Options

There are many benefits to using lease-options as a strategy to manage a portfolio of investment property. As an investor, our emphasis is to improve portfolio performance by increasing returns, reducing volatility, and lowering the overall risk.

The following characteristics make lease-options more favorable than conventional landlording:

- More Upfront Money
- Higher Rents
- Higher Sales Price
- Little or No Maintenance Costs
- Attracts Better Tenants
- Flexible Use
- Less Management Responsibilities

- Quick Tenant Removal When They Default
- Tax Benefits
- Alternative Financing

Most of these benefits come from the tenant mindset that they are "buying" a property where the lease-option becomes a form of intermediate financing for them. With this short-term intermediate financing, the goal is to obtain a refinance loan with another lender to ultimately own the property. Because of the buyer's mindset, tenants are willing to pay more and do more for the opportunity to buy.

More Upfront Money

There is almost always greater upfront money received from lease-option tenants than is normally collected with a standard rental. The tenants are willing to provide more upfront money because they view the funds they are paying as similar to a down payment in a conventional purchase with a mortgage. Because their intent is to ultimately own the property, they are willing to give extra upfront money to secure the right to purchase the property.

Higher Rents

Because few property investors are willing to sell and provide financing to the type of people we deal with, they are willing to pay a higher monthly premium for the right to buy. As such, we are able to collect higher rent payments than normally allowed through conventional rentals. It is not uncommon to receive monthly payments that are 10%-20% higher than prevailing market rents.

Higher Sales Price

In addition to the willingness to pay higher rents, the tenants are willing to pay a higher price for the property as well. The price is often secondary as long as they can afford the upfront money and the monthly rent payments.

People in this socio-economic group are simply not as discriminating in the price they pay for a property. Most are simply happy to have someone willing to sell a house to them and provide intermediate financing to do so. This sense of gratitude makes them very receptive to paying a higher price.

Little or No Maintenance Costs

When people buy houses, it is unsaid but understood that once someone buys a house, they have to assume the repair and maintenance responsibilities for that house. Because all parties are clear in the arrangement that the tenants are ultimately buying the property, it is expected they will take responsibility for all repairs and maintenance since it will become their house. To real estate investors, this point is one of the major benefits in using lease-options. Short of catastrophic damage to the property, the investor can expect nearly no maintenance or repair costs compared to those with standard rentals.

Attracts Better Tenants

The people who are attracted to lease-options are often those who have already rented for many years. They have attempted to buy a house through conventional means, but for a variety of reasons, they have been unable to do so.

Because they have rented for many years, our tenants are frustrated homebuyers looking for someone to give them an opportunity to buy with easy financing. Because many have tried to qualify for conventional mortgages, they are aware of the need for a down payment. As such, these people often have a good tenant history, are employed, and have accumulated a decent amount of savings to put towards a down payment. In our case, this is upfront money to be used for a lease-option arrangement.

Flexible Use

Typically, in a conventional rental situation, the landlord is expected to provide housing that includes functional appliances, functional environmental systems, reasonably good flooring/carpeting, landscaping, and a good interior condition. Not only are landlords expected to provide tenants this at the time of move-in, but the landlord is also expected to incur the cost of ongoing maintenance and repairs! All this so that he can collect only a small security deposit and first month's rent!

When the tenants enter into a lease-option transaction, they understand that they are "buying" into the property in "as is" condition. It does not mean that we, as investors, don't do some property preparation. However, it also doesn't mean that it is necessary to totally renovate a property before we can "sell" it. Often, you can "sell" the property "as is" with all its imperfections.

Less Management Responsibilities

Once an investment property has been "sold" through a lease-option transaction, there are almost no management responsibilities except to ensure that the monthly payment is received. The repair and maintenance responsibilities have been placed with the tenant. As such, most of the well known "landlord headaches" have been removed.

Quick Tenant Removal When They Default

The lease-option transaction, when structured correctly, often utilizes prevailing Landlord-Tenant laws of eviction to resolve cases of non-payment. With alternative forms of financing, the investor often has to resort to a foreclosure process, which can be both time-consuming and expensive.

The goal of eviction is three-fold. The first is to have the tenants removed from the property. The second is to get legal possession of the property. And the third is to get a judgment so additional collection measures, such as garnishment or levy of personal property, may be pursued.

When the tenant stops paying either voluntarily or involuntarily, having a quick repossession is paramount to getting the investment property performing again. The eviction process is the quickest and most cost-effective way to do this. With legal possession, we can take actions to once again get our investment property performing.

Tax Benefits

Monthly income from investment property under a lease-option agreement is generally considered to be rental income. Rental income generally falls under the category of "passive activity income" within the view of the IRS, which is taxed lower than personal service income (earned income).

Further, some of the upfront money collected such as security deposits can be tax-deferred until the day the landlord claims the money for compensation for damages or losses. Additionally, option money can be tax-deferred until the tenant either leaves the property or exercises the option, whichever comes first.

If the property is sold after 12 months of ownership, it is generally taxed at long-term capital gains rates, which are often much lower than earned income rates. Additionally, if advanced notice is provided, investors need not take the profits. The IRS allows property investors to do a tax-deferred "1031 exchange" so that all the profits are rolled into another property of "like-kind".

Note: As in the case of all taxation matters, you should consult a CPA or other expert financial counsel.

Alternative Financing

Many lenders and investors recognize lease-option transactions as a form of owner-financing. It gives the tenant full use of the property, but also the right to buy. This can be a favorable arrangement for both tenant and landlord. When done correctly, both parties' interests are fulfilled.

Since the lease-option transaction is often recognized as a form of owner-financing, it often facilitates greater ease in getting a new loan for the tenant so he can successfully buy the property and ultimately have title transferred into his name.

Misconceptions of Lease-Options

I often encounter investors who are conventional landlords. It seems no matter how much I try to explain the benefits of lease-option transactions to them, they never quite grasp the benefits. As such, writing this book allows me the opportunity to clarify any misconceptions.

The first step for conventional landlords is to have an open mind when it comes to investing. Never have I said, don't consider conventional landlording; it simply means by understanding lease-options, you will have an additional instrument within your investment repertoire.

Misunderstanding and resistance to lease-option transactions center on the following issues:

- The investors need for ownership "forever"
- Misunderstanding the mindset of lease-option tenants
- Ignorance of multiple profit centers

Buy and Hold Forever

People from a conventional landlording background often "buy and hold" property for life. The underlying motivation for them is to one day fully own the property "free and clear." They are primarily working for the future, and may or may not receive a lot of upfront money or monthly cash flow from their tenants. Their mindset says they are willing to sacrifice some of the money because their tenants will "pay their mortgage" until the day they own it "free and clear." They simply don't want any possibility of "losing" the property.

If the owners do hold the investment for monthly cash flow, conventional "buy and hold" investors fear they will lose the monthly income once it is sold. Along with the fear of loss of monthly income is the fear of not being able to find a replacement property.

What "buy and hold" investors fail to understand is that most people who enter into a lease-option agreement never fully exercise their option to buy. **This is not by our design.** It simply is the nature of the types of tenants that are attracted to owner-financing. They either stop paying or simply move on. If and when the property comes back to us, we can increase the upfront money, the monthly rent, and the option price to better reflect changes in the market.

This is analogous to the homebuyers of today who take on 30-year mortgages. Relatively few such mortgages live out their entire 30-year lifespan. It is commonly known in the lending industry that the average American will move every five to seven years, and when they do, they get a new 30-year loan.

Tenants who agree to lease-option agreements have the *intention* of staying with the property for a long time. However, the very reasons they were unable to buy a house conventionally are often the reasons that eventually compel them to move on. Their track record of personal stability has not been established long enough to allow them to buy conventionally.

We give our tenants the benefit of the doubt that they want to buy, but our experience has shown that most will move on within three years. Like conventional landlording, there is turnover with lease-option transactions. However, the biggest difference between the two, is that we are often financially rewarded when turnover occurs while conventional landlords are not.

Ultimately, we expect most of the houses we have in our portfolio to be paid off by our chain of lease-option tenants over the course of the next 30 years (or sooner). And on the off-chance a tenant successfully exercises his option to buy, through qualifying for a refinance loan, there is nothing difficult in rolling the realized equity forward into an equivalent replacement property.

Misunderstanding the Tenant Mindset

Generally speaking, investors who are accustomed to old-fashioned "buy and hold" often do not understand the mindset of lease-option tenants.

"Buy and hold" investors do not understand that psychologically, the desire for tenants to own a home is extremely high. It is a fundamental dream of most societies. As such, these people are willing to pay more, do more, and assume responsibility unheard of among conventional tenants.

This is the mindset that "buy and hold" investors fail to understand, but ultimately this is what translates into higher returns, better performance and fewer management challenges within our investment portfolio.

When tenants are willing to pay more and do more on all levels, it inevitably translates to better investment performance.

Tenants realize there are mostly "buy and hold" investors in the market. In the lease-options market, we have virtually no direct competition.

In my view, "buy and hold" investors miss the opportunity to capitalize on the fundamental desire of home ownership within most tenants. In many cases, it is unlikely our tenants will have the personal stability to ultimately own the property, and this often works out in our best interest.

Multiple Profit Centers

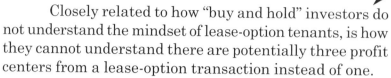

Closely related to how "buy and hold" investors do not understand the mindset of lease-option tenants, is how they cannot understand there are potentially three profit centers from a lease-option transaction instead of one.

"Buy and hold" investors are mostly focused on the monthly rents. However, in a lease-option agreement, there are potentially three profit centers.

- Upfront money
- Higher monthly payment
- Back-end Option

Typically, in a conventional rental, the upfront money received comes in the form of a security deposit and first month's rent. In the way we do lease-options, our upfront money typically consists of a security deposit, an administrative fee, prorated first month's rent, and option money.

Profit Center 1 - Upfront Money

The greater upfront money we receive from a tenant comes from their willingness to pay the equivalent of a "low down payment". The upfront money typically covers three months worth of vacancy. If we move a property within two months, we actually come out ahead with the tenant turnover.

On top of all of this, we typically do not bring the property to prime condition as we might do with a conventional rental. Later on in the book, I will explain what we do to prepare the property for "resale." I can assure you, however, that they are mostly low-expense items. Our tenants take on the responsibility of repainting, wallpapering, getting appliances, carpeting, flooring, and performing minor repairs.

It is important to note, if we subscribed only to "buy and hold," we would receive relatively little upfront money, AND we would also have to spend far more for selling the property in renovated condition.

Comparison of Lease-Option vs. Conventional Rental

3-bedroom, 1-bath house
Market Rent = $500.00, Monthly P.I.T.I. = $375.00

Lease-Option		***Conventional Rental***	
House cleaning:	$ 50.00	House cleaning:	$ 50.00
Yard care:	$ 50.00	Yard care:	$ 50.00
Carpet cleaning:	$ None	Carpet cleaning:	$ 100.00
Paint:	$ None	Paint:	$ 100.00
Appliances:	$ None	Appliances:	$ 200.00
Total Preparation Expense:	$ 100.00	Total Preparation Expense:	$ 700.00

Lease-Option preparations cost less!

Administrative Fee:	$ 200.00	Application Fee:	$ 20.00
Security Deposit:	$ 250.00	Security Deposit:	$ 350.00
Prorated 1st month:	$ 250.00	1st Month's Rent:	$ 500.00
Option Money:	$ 900.00		
Total Upfront Money:	$1,600.00	Total Upfront Money:	$ 870.00

More upfront money with a Lease-Option!

Profit Center 2 – Higher monthly payment

As I mentioned, because lease-option tenants are willing to make monthly payments that are typically higher than market rents AND are willing to take on the maintenance and repairs responsibility, we do not receive calls for such things. All we do is collect our monthly rent payments. The net effect is that we have higher monthly cash flow and no unexpected maintenance and repair expenses for the property. This is a wonderful thing.

Comparison of Lease-Option vs. Conventional Rental

3-bedroom, 1-bath house
Market Rent = $500.00, Monthly P.I.T.I. = $375.00

Lease-Option		Conventional Rental	
Tenant Payment:	$ 600.00	Tenant Payment:	$ 500.00
(-) Monthly P.I.T.I:	$ 375.00	(-) Monthly P.I.T.I.:	$ 375.00
(-) Repair & Maint:	$ None	(-) Repair & Maint:	$ 40.00
= Net Monthly Cash Flow:	$ 225.00	= Net Monthly Cash Flow:	$ 85.00
Net Annual Cash Flow:	*$2,700.00*	*Net Annual Cash Flow:*	*$1,140.00*

More spendable cash flow with a Lease-Option!

Profit Center 3 – Back-end Option

Finally, we have the option price. The price for which we sell the property is typically 10% to 20% over fair market value. The rationale for this is since we are providing the intermediate financing and bearing the risk for the next few years, we are entitled to capture the appreciation that might come along with it. However, if the tenants make substantial improvements, they receive the benefits of our commitment to cap the price. In effect, they create some "sweat equity."

One of the techniques we use to sell an imperfect or a physically distressed property is by giving a large "repairs and decoration credit." It is far easier for us to give credits on the "back-end", which may or may not be exercised, then to come up with the funds to make repairs to a property ourselves.

Not only do we receive a price higher than market value, but we also leverage this into incentive credits for our tenants to make repairs and improve the property.

As you can see, a lease-option transaction when implemented with some knowledge and creativity, can potentially have three profit centers and provide immense stability within an investor's portfolio. As an investor, the reduction of investment volatility is incredibly important.

Refinance Loan vs. New Purchase Loan

The major difference between a refinance loan and a new purchase loan is: applicants of most new purchase loans require sufficient funds for a cash down payment. (Generally 3%-20% depending on the loan program.) In addition to the cash down payment, the loan applicant must also have sufficient funds to cover "closing costs" which generally includes loan fees, broker fees, attorney fees, title research, taxes, and many other related fees. These fees are broken down in greater detail in a settlement statement and normally run into the thousands of dollars.

In a refinance loan, there are generally no down payments. The reason for this is because the lender recognizes the lease-option contract as the tenant's declaration to purchase the property in the near future. They have demonstrated this by living in the property for at least 12 months, and they have paid upfront money for a purchase option.

In the lender's eyes, as long as the tenant maintains residency and a good payment record, the tenant may be a good refinance candidate. Of course, we would like for this to occur so our tenants will get a loan to ultimately cash us out. But the tenant is still required to be responsible and clean up their personal credit.

Another benefit to our tenants in applying for a refinance loan is that nearly all closing costs are "rolled" into the loan. What this means is that all the aforementioned fees normally paid with cash for a new purchase loan are simply added to the borrowed amount of the loan. So, there is generally no upfront cash required to pay for the loan.

The cash requirement for a down payment plus closing costs often presents a big challenge for a new homebuyer. Additionally, the qualification process for a new purchase loan is generally more stringent than a refinance loan.

Summary

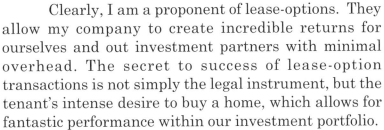

Clearly, I am a proponent of lease-options. They allow my company to create incredible returns for ourselves and out investment partners with minimal overhead. The secret to success of lease-option transactions is not simply the legal instrument, but the tenant's intense desire to buy a home, which allows for fantastic performance within our investment portfolio.

If you're looking for an innovative investment strategy, you should consider lease-options. The first step to successfully implementing lease-options is to not limit yourself to the conventional rental mindset; but keeping an open mind to alternative investment possibilities.

Written Exercise – Part 1

Did I truly understand the main points of this chapter? What do I need to review again?

Which ideas in this chapter can I adapt to my market?

Which ideas in this chapter can I start implementing immediately?

Written Exercise – Part 2

Which tasks do I need to do myself? Which tasks do I need to delegate to others?

What team members do I need to contact to assist me in implementing the ideas within this chapter?

What follow-up questions do I need to ask the Author? What additional information do I need to research?

2 The Fundamentals of Lease-Options

Basic Components of a Lease-Option Transaction

In the previous chapter, I discussed many of the benefits and underlying mindset that allows the lease-option transaction to work so well. In this chapter, I will discuss the basic components of a lease-option transaction.

At the fundamental level, there is the *lease agreement*, which allows the tenant to reside within the property in exchange for an agreed upon monthly rent payment. Then there is the *purchase option agreement.* It allows the tenant a finite amount of time to fully purchase the property at a predetermined price completing the title (ownership) transfer process.

However, this book is not meant to be a legal or technical book. It is meant to be a *practical book with practical application.* It is for the investor who wants to know how it is done, how we do it in the real world, and how it will maximize your returns.

Practically speaking, the basic components of a lease-option transaction are:

- Investment Property
- Landlord
- Tenant
- Upfront Money
- Lease Agreement
- Purchase Option Agreement
- Other Supporting Documents

Many of the components of a lease-option transaction are actually very similar to a standard rental, and with good reason! It is still fundamentally a Landlord – Tenant relationship.

Investment Property

In the context of this book, the investment properties we deal with are *single-family houses.* (All references to real estate and the real estate market are in the context of single-family houses.)

Typically, the investment property includes the land and the improvements (*the house itself*). Quite simply, the investment property is what our tenant ultimately wants. We, as investors, either control or own the investment property. The tenants not only want possession of the property; they ultimately want to take title to it, in order to claim ownership.

The landlord or property manager manages the property, although they may or may not actually have ownership interest in it.

Landlord

In the context of this book, the landlord is the property manager who oversees the day-to-day management responsibilities of the investment property and the lease-option transaction. Additionally, that person often has a limited Power of Attorney (a notarized document allowing you to appoint an individual to legally act on your behalf) to manage the affairs of the property such as: collections, insurance, financing, repairs, maintenance, evictions, and sometimes, conveyance of title.

The lease-option property manager typically has a greater breadth of responsibility than a conventional rental property manager. Like conventional rental property managers, the lease-option property manager may or may not actually have ownership interest in the property, but they certainly need to have a greater base of knowledge than the average property manager.

The term, "landlord" is being used in this book because most legal jurisdictions recognize the position and title of landlord. However, in normal business situations and interactions with contractors, lenders, insurance agents, brokers, and other professionals, we generally refer to ourselves as *property managers*.

Tenant

The tenant, of course, is the person who wants to live in and ultimately own our investment property. As I mentioned earlier, our tenant's mindset is to buy. They remain tenants until they leave the property or fully exercise their option to purchase the property. *(Please note that in the context of this book, the singular term "tenant" will be used interchangeably with the plural version "tenants" for the ease of communicating.)*

Our tenant provides the mandatory upfront money to enter into a lease-option agreement to gain possession of our property. They assume nearly all responsibilities of repair and maintenance, and when they enter into the lease-option agreement, they agree to take the property in "as is" condition.

We give our tenant autonomy and even encourage him to make cosmetic improvements to the property such as putting in appliances, carpeting, painting, flooring, wallpaper and so forth. He, of course, is responsible for all utilities and landscaping.

In a lease-option transaction, the goal of our tenant is to successfully qualify for a refinance loan from a mortgage company or some other lender, in which case, we ultimately profit from the option price already agreed upon.

Until that day arrives, however, most of our returns will come from the upfront money our tenant pays us and the ongoing monthly payments he makes.

Upfront Money

I know this may sound basic to some of you, but getting the money upfront from tenants is a very instrumental part of the entire process. I say this because I know people who have allowed tenants to sign into a lease-option agreement or have given possession to a property based on a tenant's promise to pay. This sets a dangerous precedent of giving possession to the tenant without having money to support it. This is highly inadvisable.

The way the upfront money is structured is also important. Tenants must realize there is something at risk on their end, and they must show a level of financial commitment to the property and the lease-option transaction.

Lease Agreement

The lease agreement is the most important document to us as investors and property managers. It is similar to many conventional rental agreements in that it specifies length of term, monthly rent payment, late fees, terms of default, and other tenant responsibilities. Typically, we have a one-year lease that is automatically renewable once. The net effect to the tenant is that the lease is valid for two years.

However, our lease agreement differs from traditional rental leases in many significant ways. Most notably, the lease has specially-written clauses within the agreement that state the tenant is responsible for maintenance and repairs as well as landscaping, utilities, rekeying the locks, and so forth. Furthermore, the lease allows for the tenant to make minor improvements to the property.

This lease agreement is important because it gives us the legal right to quickly and inexpensively go to court as a landlord to file for eviction and receive a judgment in the event of a breach of contract or nonpayment.

Our lease agreement provides the lease portion of the lease-option transaction and is primarily designed to protect the landlord and the investor. Additionally, our lease agreements make no mention of the purchase option agreement. When we go into court, we want the lease agreement to stand on its own merit, and not be intertwined with the purchase option agreement.

Purchase Option Agreement

The purchase option agreement is a separate document. It preserves the tenant's right to purchase the property for a set amount of time. Typically, we give a two-year purchase option. The purchase option agreement also specifies the pre-determined price of purchase upon refinance. Our option price generally captures much of the appreciation that would normally be lost through an outright sale.

In our purchase option agreement, we typically give option credits to our tenants to do painting, flooring, carpeting, decoration, and repairs. We also give additional credits for making timely rent payments.

This is a great way to encourage the tenants to build "sweat equity" for themselves by improving the property while minimizing our cash investment.

As an additional point, verbiage in the option agreement states that the validity of the option agreement is dependent upon satisfactory performance of the lease agreement. If the terms of the lease agreement are not met, then the tenant forfeits the option to buy the property. This is crucial.

Other Forms and Agreements

We have other supporting documents in addition to the core lease agreement and purchase option agreement that constitute our basic lease-option agreement.

Some of these documents include addendums to the lease and option agreement, disclosures, the security deposit agreement, appliance and inventory agreement, payment instructions, and other documents that are customized for special situations.

While the bulk of the necessary verbiage is in the core lease and option agreements, the supporting documents we use give additional credibility to further protect our position in the event it is necessary to go to court.

If you are interested in finding our more about our forms and agreements, visit *www.turnkeyinvesting.com.*

The Numbers

This section is where most investors want to spend their time looking and studying; and with good reason! We discuss specifics as to how the numbers work and make large returns with lease-options.

As you will see from our examples, there are many variables that impact the bottom-line number. The truth of the matter is, the charts provide simplified examples. There are actually more cost and profit factors within each lease-option transaction we do.

Occasionally, there are "hidden" and unexpected costs that occur. The good news is that we also benefit unexpectedly when financing is more favorable than we expect or the holding costs are lower than we anticipate.

The point of showing this example is to simply illustrate the most significant numbers along with factors we look at during the buying and selling process. It is the combined results of the entire buying, marketing, and selling process that produce the cash flow and phenomenal returns we receive.

Using Conventional Financing

This example shows how our lease-option numbers work with conventional financing. I define conventional financing as the investment loans most investors have to qualify for with a mortgage company or a bank.

Using Bank Financing

"BUY"

Fair Market Value:	**$50,000**	**30-year Finance @ 7% interest**	
Purchase Price:	$45,000	Mortgage Pymt:	$266.33
(-) 10% Down:	$ 5,000	Taxes & Insurance:	$ 99.67
= 90% Finance:	$40,000	Total P.I.T.I.:	$366.00

Closing Costs: $ 2,000
(Additional cash)

Our Holding Costs (2 months)

P.I.T.I.:	$ 732.00
Marketing:	$ 300.00
Total Holding:	$1,032.00

"SELL"

"Owner-Financing" with Lease-Option

Option Price:	$60,000	Tenant's Monthly Pymt:	$ 600.00
(-) Upfront Money:	$ 1,600		
= Refinance Price:	$58,400		

Contract Equity Position:	*$13,400.00*
Total Cash Investment:	*$ 8,032.00*
Net Cash Investment:	*$ 6,432.00*
Net Cash flow:	*$234.00/month*
Annual cash flow:	*$ 2,808.00*
Cash-on-Cash Returns:	***43.6%***

Better returns than savings accounts, certificates of deposits (CDs), mutual funds, and most stocks!

After you study the example, I would like to make a few comments.

Purchase Price

We are buying a property valued at $50,000 for a 10% discount which accounts for the purchase price of $45,000. It is not uncommon for us to get bigger discounts than the 10% we minimally look for. However, we have chosen a more conservative number to illustrate that the numbers still work in our favor.

Financing

We assume a standard 10% down plus closing costs for a conventional 30-year investment loan at 7% interest. In recent years, interest rates have dropped to phenomenally low rates. However, we prefer to use a more conservative rate in calculations. With bank financing, we also have closing costs that are in addition to the down payment.

P.I.T.I.

P.I.T.I. stands for Principal, Interest, Taxes, and Insurance. These are the principal items within every standard mortgage payment. It represents our monthly fixed cost of owning the property, and it must be paid at all times even during times of vacancy.

Holding Costs

We always assume there are vacancy and marketing costs when we acquire a new property. Our average hold time is less than two months, but we use the entire two months for ease of calculations. Some properties take up to four months to sell; others are sold within days. From a portfolio view, using two months works best for us.

Resale Price

With every property we sell, we mark every property up for resale at least $10,000 above the fair market value of the house, not what we paid for it. Based on the example, that is a 20% markup. Remember, despite the fact we bought the property for less than fair market value, it is still worth fair market value. And because our tenants will not cash us out until two or more years later, we capture that future appreciation for ourselves by marking up the option price.

Upfront Money

This is the total money we expect to receive from a new lease-option tenant. It will eventually offset some of the money initially invested to purchase and hold the property.

Tenant's Monthly Payment

This payment is set by our lease and is often higher than prevailing market rents under a conventional rental arrangement. Why? As I said before, our tenants are willing to pay more for the right to purchase.

Contract Equity Position

This number is strictly for internal use and a way to gauge the starting "paper" position of the investment. This equity is what we have "created" through a lease-option contract. It is not realized until a tenant gets a new loan and exercises the purchase option.

Total Cash Investment

This is the total upfront cash the investor committed to purchase and hold the property. It includes the down payment, closing costs, and holding costs.

Net Cash Investment

This is the Total Cash Investment the investor made minus the upfront money received from our new tenants. The upfront money both offsets and helps us recover the Total Cash Investment.

Cash Flow

Our Net Cash Flow is our Tenant's Monthly Payment minus our monthly P.I.T.I. In effect, it is our spendable monthly profit for that one property. The Annual Cash Flow is the Net Cash Flow multiplied by 12 months.

Cash-on-Cash Returns

This is our bottom line number and serves as a benchmark to how that investment property will perform if all goes according to plan. However, it does not take into account the short-term risk and impact to a portfolio when vacancies or unexpected expenses occur. As an evaluation tool, it is often very effective.

The subtitle of this book is *"How to Simply and Safely Create 12% Returns with Investment Property!"* I think you can see that with this first example, I more than deliver my promise.

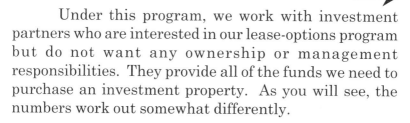

Using Private Financing

Under this program, we work with investment partners who are interested in our lease-options program but do not want any ownership or management responsibilities. They provide all of the funds we need to purchase an investment property. As you will see, the numbers work out somewhat differently.

Using Private Financing

"BUY"

Fair Market Value:	**$50,000**	**5-Year Loan @ 10% interest**	
Purchase Price:	$42,500	Interest-only Pymt:	$354.17
(-) 0% Down:	$ zero	Taxes & Insurance:	$ 95.83
= 100% Finance:	$42,500	Total I.T.I.:	$450.00

Closing Costs: $ 450
(Additional cash)

Our Holding Costs (2 months)

I.T.I.:	$ 900.00
Marketing:	$ 300.00
Total Holding:	$1,200.00

"SELL"

"Owner-Financing" with Lease-Option

Option Price:	$60,000	Tenant's Monthly Pymt:	$ 600.00
(-) Upfront Money:	$ 1,600		
= Refinance Price:	$58,400		

Contract Equity Position:	*$13,400.00*
Total Cash Investment:	*$ 1,650.00*
Net Cash Investment:	*$ 50.00*
Net Cash flow:	*$150.00/month*
Annual cash flow:	*$ 1,800.00*
Cash-on-Cash Returns:	***3,600.0%***

Returns are off the scale with no basis of comparison!

There are some notable differences in how using private financing impacts our lease-option transaction.

Purchase Price

Because we are buying with "all cash", it allows us greater negotiating power to get a larger discount. As such, our purchase price is somewhat lower than the purchase price we would pay with conventional bank financing.

I would also like to point out that our discounts off the purchase price can be deeper with "all cash" offers. But for the sake of conservatism, I have chosen a less discounted price to illustrate the fact that the numbers still work well with a lesser discount.

Financing

The financing we use comes from the liquid funds our investment partners provide. In essence, we get 100% financing to purchase the property.

Our investment partners demand a higher return on their money than banks and other conventional lenders do. In this example, we pay 10% returns in the form of interest-only payments. Our investment partners have their funds secured and collateralized by a first mortgage position on the property that has built-in equity.

As we make interest-only payments for the next five years, our investment partners can evaluate our performance and consider whether they want to redeem their investment funds or renew their investment for another five years. In essence, we create a program very similar to a 5-year certificate of deposit except they receive much better returns than any bank can offer.

Alternatively, investment partners can tap into their retirement funds and participate in our program. However, it does require an administrator who is experienced in such programs and transactions. We know reputable people who are both knowledgeable and experienced in using retirement funds to invest in real estate.

Closing Costs

Our closing costs in this scenario are low because we are only paying our attorney to coordinate this type of closing.

Holding Costs

Our holding time remain the same as our Conventional Financing example. The way we market our properties is not impacted by how we buy the investment property.

Sell Terms

All of our sell terms are also identical to the Conventional Financing example. Please refer to the commentary in the Conventional Financing section.

The Returns

Despite the fact that our cash flow in this scenario is actually lower, our cash-on-cash returns are higher. Further, because of the mathematical peculiarity of how little cash we have in the investment, it causes the cash-on-cash returns to be "off the scale". In some respects, this deal actually has more financial risk in the fact that our underlying monthly commitment (the taxes and interest payment) is higher. Despite this, the investment partner's interest in this investment is still quite secure because of the built-in equity in the collateral property.

"Textbook" Transactions

The examples we provided are average "textbook" transactions in our area. There are houses we buy that are both higher in price and lower in price than shown in our examples. Every investment is different, and we take special care to evaluate each investment property on its own merits.

Using Seller-Financing

Another option not illustrated with a diagram is seller-financing. Frequently we buy investment properties with financing already in place. We buy from distressed sellers who have gotten behind in their payments or need a quick sale.

We buy it quickly by having the title of the property transferred to us and paying the equity the sellers have (if any) in cash. We then resume making timely monthly payments. We do this without qualifying for a new loan or formally assuming the loan.

This method of property acquisition we do is referred to as a "subject to" purchase. This means we are buying the property "subject to" the terms of the existing mortgage. The specifics of how we do this and nuances of these types of transactions are far beyond the scope of this book.

The overall investment returns using Seller-Financing can vary greatly between examples shown with Conventional Financing and those with Private Financing.

Sometimes, there is a substantial amount of cash we must invest to take advantage of seller-financing. In which case, the cash-on-cash returns are similar to Conventional Financing. Other times, there is very little cash required, and the cash-on-cash returns are "off the scale" similar to Private Financing.

I have not presented an example here because there is no such thing as a "textbook example". When buying investment property with Seller-Financing, it is largely done on a case-by-case basis.

Beyond the Technical Components

Beyond the technical components are the less quantifiable, but very important aspects of a lease-option transaction, which include:

- Tenant Mindset
- Real Estate Market
- Legal Environment
- Marketing & Advertising
- Administration
- Management Philosophy

Each of these topics is covered in greater detail in later chapters of this book, but for the purpose of this chapter, I will provide a brief description of why each is essential to every lease-option transaction.

Tenant Mindset

Having spoken to many beginning investors in the last few years, I have learned that one of the most difficult challenges they face is understanding the mindset of the tenants we deal with. Beginning investors from an affluent socio-economic background, find it difficult to understand the priorities and needs of our lower middle-class, "blue-collar" tenants.

As such, they often sabotage the process by imposing their values on their tenants by selecting "nicer" properties which are similar to something the investors, themselves, would live in, but are not necessarily financially viable alternatives for the prospective tenants. They may also try to renovate the property to a state of "newness," or bring up issues such as mortgage tax deductions, which have no bearing or importance to the type of tenants we serve. Not understanding the tenant mindset can lead to the investment property not performing as well as it should.

Real Estate Market

The real estate market in the context of lease-options refers to the housing market in which you plan to invest. *(Throughout this book, the housing market I work and invest in is the Columbus, Georgia and Phenix City, Alabama area.)*

Important aspects of a housing market can include the demand and price of residential properties, the demand and rent rates for rental housing, and the relationship of rent rates to mortgage payments when purchasing an investment property.

These are very important factors to investigate and do market assessments on, prior to using the lease-option strategy with investment properties. Without the proper market research, even the best executed lease-option transactions will ultimately become unprofitable.

More about real estate market research and assessment is covered in Chapter 3.

Legal Environment

The legal environment in which you invest can determine the long-term success of utilizing the lease-option technique as an investment strategy. The legal environment refers to whether or not the municipalities in which you operate have Landlord-Tenant laws that are investor-friendly (landlord-friendly) or tenant-friendly.

Fundamentally, the lease-option strategy is largely dependent upon Landlord-Tenant laws for enforcement of the terms of the lease. More specifically, is it possible to quickly and easily evict tenants if and when they do not perform? Environments that are not investor-friendly are areas in which I would not recommend executing lease-options as an investment strategy.

The other part of the legal environment that must be investigated is whether incorporation laws are business-friendly or not. There are some states in the U.S. where incorporation brings about significant administrative challenges and costs. In other states, incorporation is easy and inexpensive. The issue of incorporation becomes important for the purposes of taxation and asset protection.

More about assessing the legal environment is covered in Chapter 3.

Marketing & Advertising

While it may seem strange to include marketing and advertising as an essential component of implementing lease-options, it is nevertheless a very important part of the process. Without a solid marketing plan to attract the right tenants and to educate the public about what we offer, just about any investment property will either sit vacant for long periods of time, or simply not perform well at all.

One of the ways we improve the performance of our investment portfolio is by having a visible, consistent and ongoing advertising campaign in our community. Good marketing and advertising can overcome potential losses from property imperfections, vacancy, and evictions.

More on Marketing and Advertising is covered in Chapter 6.

Administration

Unlike stock investments, overseeing a real estate portfolio is far more demanding. But it can also be far more rewarding. There is generally more control in owning a real estate portfolio than in having a stock portfolio.

In a real estate portfolio, the overhead and administrative responsibilities are far more daunting. There are property taxes, insurance, purchase contracts, evictions, bank deposits, mortgage payments, appraisals, lease agreements, etc. Owning and managing a real estate portfolio, even with the lease-option strategy, can generate a lot of paperwork. In fact, if the investment portfolio is large enough, you may need to hire or work with a property manager or bookkeeper to coordinate all the administrative issues that come with each and every investment property you acquire.

Being able to effectively deal with administration is essential in managing a real estate investment portfolio. More on the subject of administration is covered in Chapter 10.

Management Philosophy

The concept of management philosophy is somewhat esoteric in a real estate book, but it is important nonetheless. The management philosophy drives the actions, decisions, and execution of any business or investment. The management philosophy can improve or damage the performance of any investment portfolio. This is especially true when we seek investment property and utilize the lease-option strategy to create good returns on our investment portfolio.

We have a particular management philosophy we follow as part of our Turnkey Investing Philosophy. More of this is covered in Chapter 11.

The 6 "S"s of TurnKey Investing

TurnKey Investing is about the 6 basic values that guide what we do. Each of these fundamental values exists within our preferred method of real estate investing: the Lease-Options Strategy.

Simple

For investing to be a turnkey system, it has to be *simple to understand* and *simple to implement*. Most importantly, it has to be *simple to invest* in.

Safety

Turnkey investing is about *safety*, not speculation or "sexiness" of the idea. Turnkey investing creates *safety* through experience, certainty, and risk management.

Steady

Turnkey investing is about delivering *steady performance*. It is about carrying out essential activities in an even-keeled, consistently, steady way. It is about avoiding dazzle and drama in the day-to-day activities.

Security

The way we protect our investment partners in turnkey investing is about offering *security (collateral)*, not just a promise or a good story. With real estate, the investment property is often the back-end security to a *secure* investment plan.

Spendable

Within our investment portfolio, our turnkey investments generate *spendable cash flow* each and every month. This is not perceived equity or compounding the returns. We create *spendable returns* for ourselves and our investment partners. They can *choose* how to deploy the spendable returns they receive.

Systems

Turnkey investing is about creating and developing a *duplicatable system* of tasks that can be used over and over. We create and execute a *management, marketing, and investing system* with a turnkey philosophy in mind.

Summary

This chapter outlines the fundamentals of lease-options. There are basic components to every lease-option transaction, and these components are customized to each situation. Understanding the fundamentals of lease-options serves as the basis of discussion for the remainder of this book.

As with any investment, there is a process to financial calculations to determine the feasibility and potential profitability of any lease-optioned property. We have outlined ours in this chapter as the net result of both buying and selling of the property. It is both quantifiable and measurable. It is an important tool to use in evaluating any investment property.

The lease-option investment strategy is more than its technical components. There is an entire management mindset that goes with it. The following chapters outline and describe the entire lease-option process from an investor and property management perspective from beginning to end.

Written Exercise – Part 1

Did I truly understand the main points of this chapter? What do I need to review again?

Which ideas in this chapter can I adapt to my market?

Which ideas in this chapter can I start implementing immediately?

Written Exercise – Part 2

Which tasks do I need to do myself? Which tasks do I need to delegate to others?

What team members do I need to contact to assist me in implementing the ideas within this chapter?

What follow-up questions do I need to ask the Author? What additional information do I need to research?

3 How to Research the Market

Assessing the Market

With every type of business or investment, it is absolutely necessary to conduct thorough market research and assessment into the business, economic, and legal environment in which you plan to operate.

It has often been said, "no man is an island" and "people don't operate in a vacuum." In other words, the market we work within impacts us; being aware of our economic environment is essential. When building an investment portfolio, this is especially true.

The market research involved in successfully implementing lease-options generally fall into the following categories:

- Real Estate Market
- Legal Environment

When researching the real estate market, I look at the following factors:

- Market Rents
- Fair Market Value of "Working-Class" Houses
- Market Velocity
- Appreciation

Market Rents

At the core of every lease-option transaction, we determine the maximum monthly payment we can charge our tenants for each property. In order to determine this, research into the going rental rates is vital.

Although data from real estate agencies can be helpful, I prefer to get my figures directly from the rental market at large. I find real estate agencies don't always do what is best for their client property owners. They do what is convenient for them.

The most accessible source is the local newspaper, where the terms of rent for houses, duplexes, triplexes, and apartments can easily be found.

Although the context of this book is implementing lease-options with single-family homes, I am very aware there are competitive forces coming from apartments and other housing units. Although we can and do charge more than market rents for our properties, our tenants are still sensitive to the monthly payments they have to pay. There is a limit to how far above market rents they are willing to go.

No Fancy Formulas

As much as we like formulas, we simply don't use them. We use our knowledge, field experience, and even our sense of intuition to set our rents. The reason we do this is because some properties truly defy logic (both positively and negatively). When we discover this about certain properties, we may not know the cause, but we go with how the market responds to the property and our marketing.

Rental Rates in Different Parts of Town

Because every city has its own set of regional characteristics, it is not enough to simply look at what the overall average rents go for in the city. Instead, we look regionally within the city itself. For example, in the city of Columbus, Georgia, we know the south side is the less desirable part of town. It consists of older homes and is closer to the military base of Ft. Benning. Here, rents are lower and many properties are smaller, older, and have more wear and tear.

On the flip side, we know the north side of town is favorable to newer developments and newer homes. It is where many of the affluent and professional population live. It is where most of us would prefer to live but it is an area where we do not invest!

Towards the downtown area, there are pockets of both low-income and high-income housing. It varies from neighborhood to neighborhood and cannot be easily categorized.

Whether it is the east, west, north, or south side of town, there are concentrations of apartment rentals in each, and the rents are largely consistent and commensurate for the immediate area.

We investigate all areas, make important distinctions as to what is occurring in each market rental, and keep track of the findings. By gathering the necessary data and making the appropriate distinctions for the market, we determine what market rents should be charged for any given investment property.

The Occasional Guessing Game

Occasionally, no matter how much research we do, we inevitably run into a property that will require us to do make an educated guess. This means we make an estimate and simply advertise it to "test" the market. If our rents are too high and demand is low, we will know based on the volume of calls and interest we receive. If we estimate the rents correctly, then ongoing activity and interest for the property will be strong.

The Ideal City Size

Several years ago when I moved from Atlanta to Columbus, it was both a personal and professional choice. After buying a few properties, I chose to no longer participate in the Atlanta market. The city was too large for me to be able to fully assess the investment market. Also, there were too many business and economic forces at work than I could comfortably monitor.

Although I could have chosen to work in one small region of Atlanta, I knew any region were subject to the goings-on of the entire metropolitan area. I wanted the ability to work and learn the entire market, which was possible in a smaller city like Columbus.

The metropolitan area we work in primarily consists of the cities of Columbus, Georgia and Phenix City, Alabama. The two cities combined boast a population of over 200,000. I recommend working in a city with a population between 100,000 and 300,000. The market is small enough to master, but large and diverse enough to support a large portfolio of investment property.

With this population base, you can comfortably assess market rents and work most of the rental markets within a city.

In the Appendix sections, we have in-depth demographic information on the two cities we work in. The information I have compiled came directly from the 2000 U.S. Census.

Market Value of "Working-Class" Houses

Another important criterion in selecting an area in which to build an investment portfolio is to determine what are the average prices for "working-class" houses. More specifically, what are the market values of houses "blue-collar", working-class citizens live in?

In my research of Columbus, these houses fall into the $50,000 to $65,000 range. This does not mean some of these citizens do not live in houses that are lower than $50,000 or higher than $65,000. It simply means we favor and focus on houses in this price range.

These houses fit into what we call the "sweet spot." We define the "sweet spot" as the optimal balance of desirability, size and price for our tenants, ***versus*** the price, risk levels, capital investment and cash flow we prefer as investors.

The "sweet spot" will vary from market to market and will be influenced by investor preferences and risk tolerance.

Having a lower purchase price for investment property often means you can build a larger investment portfolio with somewhat less risk. In effect, you get more properties for less capital and investment.

Market Velocity

Every market has a "speed" at which it operates. I call this "speed" the *market velocity*. For example, during the late 1990's during the dot-com craze, the market velocity was unbelievably quick in many areas of California. As the saying goes, houses sold like hotcakes! Houses were listed and sold in a matter of days, sometimes hours!

Markets that experience high market velocity are often referred to as "hot markets." And while hot markets ensure properties are sold or rented quickly, they often present challenges for investors who are looking to acquire property for their investment portfolio that will produce cash flow vs. those that produce capital gains.

Part of building an investment portfolio is knowing what objectives you want to accomplish. For me, maximizing cash flow while lowering my cost of entry is very important. By lowering the cost of entry, I automatically lower my risk per investment property.

When I was in Atlanta several years ago, the same working-class houses that cost $75,000 to $85,000 *then*, only cost $50,000 to $65,000 **today** in Columbus! As you can see, there is a significant difference in price. Additionally, the net cash flow I received was relatively smaller, and my cost of investment entry was higher.

In Columbus, the average selling time (otherwise known as Days on the Market) is four months. And while many of you may gasp at this, this figure is based on how real estate agents sell houses; it includes the entire process of finding a buyer who can fully qualify for a mortgage and close successfully.

Remember, the whole premise of what we do is to provide "owner-financing" to our tenants. As such, the criteria to enter into one of our lease-option contracts are far easier to qualify for, than a traditional mortgage.

Because of this, we often move properties in less than two months. On very few occasions, do we have properties that take four full months to move.

Today, we have the #1 position as providers of owner-financed houses. We have built-in momentum that allows us to sell a house literally within two weeks of a property coming on the market. I know this may not be impressive for anyone living in California. But in this part of the country, it is very impressive and nearly unheard of.

Despite the slower market velocity of the metro-Columbus area, we consistently and significantly beat the averages in our sales record. The velocity within our niche is far quicker than the overall market velocity. We take pride in this. Because of this, we are rarely concerned with the occasional property that is vacant longer than usual.

Even though we consistently beat the average market velocity, it is still an important benchmark for us to monitor. That benchmark helps us to evaluate our own performance.

Appreciation

A common criterion that many investors look for within investment property is the appreciation factor. Appreciation is the ongoing price inflation of property. It generally means the overall demand for property is increasing. Let me say, I have nothing against property appreciation; it is generally a good thing. However, having studied highly appreciating markets, there are also some negative consequences and undesirable side effects.

The purpose of lease-optioning property is primarily to produce cash flow safely and reliably with minimal management hassles and costs, not necessarily to profit from appreciation.

While it is possible to implement lease-options anywhere in the U.S., some areas are more favorable than others. Trying to produce cash flow from properties in highly-appreciating areas is often challenging from a numbers point of view.

Even if you do receive positive cash flow from properties in highly-appreciating areas, the risk you have to take to get the cash flow is often higher. The safety of producing cash flow is reduced when the underlying payments to buy a property is disproportionally high for the returns being made.

Another reason to lease-option a property is to have the ability to profit from a backend sale where the option price is above market value. In a highly-appreciating area, the value of a property could conceivably outstrip the option price that was set. You would be compelled to sell your property at a lower price than market value. This defeats the purpose of setting an option price from an investor's point of view.

In these cases, it might be more profitable to simply do a conventional rental to preserve the equity position. In fact, I have friends in high appreciating markets that do just that.

The Impact of Appreciation

Another side effect of lease-optioning property in a highly-appreciating area is it increases the likelihood of a refinance by tenants. The rapidly-appreciating property allows the tenant to more easily qualify for a refinance, since the market value of the property will likely outstrip the option price.

Depending on your investment objectives, having a refinance may not be favored especially since there may be negative tax ramifications in receiving the capital gains. With a refinance, it could be advantageous for us to do a 1031 Tax exchange in order to defer the taxes. *(Note: We are not tax experts in this area; be sure to consult someone well-versed who will guide you appropriately.)*

If long-term cash flow is the objective of an investment, rampant appreciation can undermine the effects of a lease-option. Thus, even as a proponent of the lease-option strategy, I do not think it is appropriate in all real estate markets or in all situations.

I do market research to see what the appreciation rate is for the typical working-class house. Then, I look at the cost of buying the house as well the monthly mortgage payment, and these are compared against the rental rates. If the positive cash flow is not large enough or it is negative cash flow, then I know lease-optioning property in a particular area is not practical.

This does not mean you cannot invest in lease-optioned property; it simply means you may have to buy property in a different geographical area and work with a management team experienced in such matters. Think out of the box and investigate new uncultivated market areas.

Legal Environment

When performing the market research and assessing the legal environment to determine if implementing lease-option transactions is practical or favorable, I look at the following areas:

- Landlord-Tenant Laws
- Incorporation Laws

By far the most important legal aspect I look at in determining whether I would lease-option property in a given area is my understanding of local Landlord-Tenant laws and the procedures for eviction and winning a civil case.

Landlord-Tenant Laws

What I look for in Landlord-Tenant laws occasionally varies. But generally, I look at the financial costs of getting a tenant out, and how quickly and easily they can be removed in a non-payment situation. Eviction filing costs vary greatly, and clearly, it goes without saying — the less expensive, the better.

The amount of time between filing and serving the tenant is also important. Some areas have huge case backlogs. What this means is that a vacancy cost is incurred by the sheer act of waiting for the court system. Also, the tenant is generally allowed a predetermined amount of time to reply. In our area, it is generally seven days. If they do reply, then a court date is generally set. And whether we win by default (no tenant response) or by judgment, loss of time is incurred.

The objective is to find out how quickly we can gain full legal possession of the property so we can prepare the property for re-marketing to make it a performing asset once again.

The point of this section is not to attempt to teach all the nuances of Landlord-Tenant laws. There are entire books written on this. As investors, we need to understand the broad strokes of ease, cost, and turnaround time. There are plenty of excellent landlord books available at your favorite online or neighborhood bookstore. You can find a list of those books I recommend in the Recommended Resources section in the back of this book.

Pro-Landlord or Pro-Tenant?

Another aspect of looking at Landlord-Tenant laws is determining whether the local court system tends to favor the landlord or the tenant. This is not generally found in any book, but rather by researching the reputation of the judge or local court system.

There are a few ways to do this. One is to simply call the courthouse and find out when eviction hearings occur and then attend the various cases. Another is to talk to a local real estate attorney who has experience in evictions. The third way is to ask other landlords, investors, or property managers in the area and learn from their experience.

The whole idea behind this is to find out the general reputation. Landlords and property managers will generally provide the strongest and quickest information you need.

I like to hear things like: "Filing for eviction is easy." "Filing for eviction is inexpensive." "The courts serve the papers fast." "The judge doesn't waste time telling the tenant to move out if they haven't paid." "The judge doesn't like to hear tenant excuses. He has heard it all before." Having a friendly, landlord environment within the court system is a must for a successful lease-option portfolio.

Incorporation Laws

For those investors with larger portfolios, we recommend placing property into a corporate entity for privacy, taxation, and asset protection reasons. Working within a state that is pro-business and encourages new business will have favorable corporation organization rules and regulations.

Favorable means it is relatively easy to set up new legal entities such as LLC's, limited partnerships, corporations, etc. Also, setup costs are relatively inexpensive, and the annual maintenance and reporting costs are nominal.

Again, I bring this up as an issue of consideration for anyone wanting to own or manage a portfolio of property. However, the discussion of which corporate structure to use is beyond the scope of this book and certainly beyond our field of expertise.

Summary

As with any business endeavor, lease-optioning of property for cash flow requires in-depth market research to determine the feasibility and profitability of the venture. There are locations, market conditions, economic and legal environments that lend themselves more favorably to using the lease-option strategy than others. Investing in an area without the necessary market assessment market could result in disastrous financial results.

If you need assistance in market assessments, please contact us at *www.turnkeyinvesting.com*.

Written Exercise – Part 1

Did I truly understand the main points of this chapter? What do I need to review again?

Which ideas in this chapter can I adapt to my market?

Which ideas in this chapter can I start implementing immediately?

Written Exercise – Part 2

Which tasks do I need to do myself? Which tasks do I need to delegate to others?

What team members do I need to contact to assist me in implementing the ideas within this chapter?

What follow-up questions do I need to ask the Author? What additional information do I need to research?

4 Purchasing Investment Properties

In this chapter, I will explain how we evaluate and determine which properties are suitable for the lease-option strategy. As previously mentioned, our findings are largely based on our geographical area and market only.

Several years ago before I left Atlanta, I did a lot of market research in several real estate markets in the southeast U.S. There was nothing inherently special about the southeast except that I had developed a familiarity with the area (in particular Georgia), the culture, and I did not want to make my business more complicated by moving out of the region.

My Initial Strategy

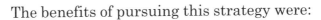

The benefits of pursuing this strategy were:

- The cost of entry for each investment property would be significantly lower thus reducing the risk per investment.

- My exposure with monthly payments was lower when vacancies occurred.
- It was easier to learn and become knowledgeable about a smaller city than a larger one.
- Armed with my knowledge and the abundance of good investment property, I could more easily become the dominant provider of owner-financed properties *(using lease-options).*
- A slower, less competitive market would make property acquisitions easier.

Coming from the hot market of Atlanta where there were literally hundreds of property investors buying and selling property, it seemed far more attractive to move into a smaller city where there were relatively few investors buying property to lease-option out.

It is important to realize that although we market our properties with the term "owner-financing", the lease-option strategy is still fundamentally tied to the local housing market, more specifically, conventional rentals.

In my initial market research, I looked at rental rates of apartments in different parts of the city. I also looked at rentals for three-bedroom houses. But for the most part, there were often not enough rental houses in any one area to decidedly determine what market rents were. Because of lack of competition, there is greater flexibility in setting a monthly rental rate for three-bedroom houses because the baseline sample of comparison is less than apartments.

Nevertheless, there is still a limit to how aggressively we can price a house.

Purchase Criteria

These are some of the purchase criteria we set when we buy:

- Avoid Bad Neighborhoods
- Avoid Major Renovations
- Buy in "Blue-Collar" Neighborhoods
- Avoid Buying in "White-Collar" Neighborhoods

Avoid Bad Neighborhoods

We do not buy in "bad" neighborhoods which are known to either have a high crime rate or where drugs are rampant. Of course, there aren't any neighborhoods (even the affluent ones) that are entirely crime-free or drug-free. But neighborhoods which have a notorious reputation for high crime rates and high drug-trafficking, we absolutely avoid.

The biggest reason we avoid these neighborhoods is that no property is worth risking bodily harm to our tenants or ourselves. And if we acquire properties in a dangerous area, we may find difficulties renting or selling the property no matter how much we lower the price.

Avoid Major Renovations

Next, we generally buy properties that have few structural problems. If they are only cosmetically unappealing, we will consider the property. Examples of what we consider major structural problems are: foundation cracks or having to replace the roof, entire walls, plumbing, or electrical wiring. These are major projects that require more time, effort, and management than we are willing to take on.

We are not renovators or "rehabbers" of property, so we avoid those types of property.

Cosmetically-challenged properties are still marketable utilizing very little extra funds. The insights and process of how we do this is covered in a Chapter 5.

In theory, any type of property can potentially be lease-optioned out. However, the location and type of property we buy often dictates the type of person it attracts.

Buy in "Blue-Collar" Neighborhoods

We like to target the lower, middle-class group of people also known as "blue-collar" workers or the "working-class". We prefer this group of people because they are largely ignored and have been given a lower priority status by most lenders. Buying a house for themselves is very challenging because they often have little credit, damaged credit, or problem credit. They are also less educated in the home-buying process.

Because of these reasons, the blue-collar group is generally more flexible in what house they will accept. The ease and ability to get financing to buy a home is often more important than cosmetic challenges they might encounter. More importantly, they are generally more appreciative of the opportunity to buy a house in "as is" condition rather than picking out the imperfections of a house. Cosmetic imperfections and even minor structural problems are often things our tenants are willing to "fix up" for themselves.

Avoid Buying in "White-Collar" Neighborhoods

Another benefit of serving blue-collar tenants is they are generally less sophisticated buyers. There are potentially fewer legal challenges if there are disagreements or disputes. These tenants generally can't afford to seek attorneys for legal representation or don't know how to file lawsuits for disagreements they may have.

Compare this mindset to the more affluent, upper middle-class group of people. They are generally professional, "white-collar" workers, who tend to be more sophisticated and have more housing options. And even if they are credit-challenged, they often have higher expectations and higher demands of the property and the entire transaction. In short, they are pickier and much harder to please.

These people tend to be higher educated and know how to "work the system." As such, if they experience problems or are disgruntled with management, they are more likely to seek an attorney for legal representation or file a lawsuit. In the case of eviction, they can potentially draw the process out.

Part of our ongoing success is to take preventive measures by selecting the clientele we want to work with and those we prefer not to. The type of houses we buy greatly influence the tenants we attract.

This group tends to be less appreciative of "owner-financing" with the lease-option arrangement. Because their view is "settling for what they can get" vs. being appreciative of the opportunity, it's a totally different tenant mindset.

Because of the blue-collar demographic we prefer to deal with, we generally purchase properties that attract these people. As it turns out, properties that accommodate this profile also have the optimal balance of financial reward vs. investment risk.

Purchase Methods

There are various ways to purchase a property, and the way we purchase a property can influence the price we pay for it.

Some ways to purchase property include:

- Seller-financing
- Conventional financing
- Private financing

Seller-Financing

If we buy a property with seller-financing and minimal cash, we are able to be more flexible on price. In fact, we can almost pay "full price" for a property and still do well. How? Because it becomes largely a "sign and buy" type of arrangement. The original owner allows us to step in, take over their existing financing, and make payments right where they left off.

Often, we buy property from people in various stages of preforeclosure where they need someone to not only take over the financing and the property, but someone must pay the arrears as well.

Buying with seller-financing is favorable to us for a number of reasons:

- Since we are not getting a new loan, there are no loan fees or down payment. We take over the current loan and simply make payments.

- We bypass the time-consuming qualification process since we are not getting a new loan. The closing is quick and inexpensive.

With these benefits, we can "afford" to pay more for the property than we normally would if we had to go through a conventional mortgage loan process.

The downside of this method is that relatively few sellers will allow others to take over their financing. For every property we buy in this way, there may be 20 others who said no, or where it simply didn't make financial sense for us to move forward.

Creative financing and purchasing discussions are beyond the scope of this book. Suffice it to say, how we buy a property can influence our decision whether to buy at all, especially where a property has very little equity.

Conventional Financing

The most common way many investors buy property is to qualify for a new conventional loan through a bank or other mortgage lender. Under this method, there is usually at least a 10% down payment plus closing costs. The major benefit to using conventional financing is the ability to buy nearly any property with a favorable interest rate as long you qualify for the loan.

The downside of buying this way is there is a limit to how many loans any one investor can qualify for. Lenders and bankers become nervous when there are too many mortgage loans outstanding for any one individual especially when it comes to single-family houses.

Private Financing

Using private financing through investment partners is the method we now prefer. There are several advantages to buying property with private financing:

- Larger equity positions can be acquired
- No loan qualification process
- Quick, easy, and inexpensive closings
- Funds from retirement accounts can be used to purchase investment property
- Higher returns than 5-year certificates of deposits.

Buying with "all cash" through private financing enables large equity positions to be acquired, since there is a considerable amount of power in "all cash" offer. More importantly, many affluent investors dislike having to sign for loans, especially for investment property that others manage. They would rather use cash so they don't take a credit hit, and they need not worry about the cumbersome loan qualification process.

Foreign investors cannot easily qualify for loans in the U.S. As such, using private financing allows them to easily invest in property that they would not otherwise be able to do if they had to qualify for a loan.

For people who have substantial retirement accounts and want to use those funds to invest in real estate, it is far less complicated to use cash funds from a retirement account than to bring financing into the picture.

Additionally, many people have some of their liquid funds in low-paying 5-year certificates of deposits or money market accounts. They receive a substantially higher return by investing in a lease-option program than have the money parked in some low-paying bank account.

Property Insurance

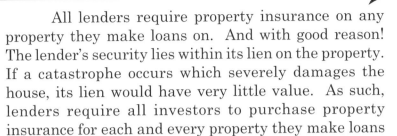

All lenders require property insurance on any property they make loans on. And with good reason! The lender's security lies within its lien on the property. If a catastrophe occurs which severely damages the house, its lien would have very little value. As such, lenders require all investors to purchase property insurance for each and every property they make loans on.

Even without a lender's requirement, it still makes good business sense to have property insurance. The relatively small cost of monthly insurance premiums covering an entire property against catastrophic loss is well worth it.

The specific type of property insurance we buy varies from property to property. In our area, it is largely influenced by fire department coverage. In other words, the better the coverage from a fire department, the more savings we will receive on our premiums.

We generally buy landlord policies for investment property. Sometimes we buy Fire policies only. Landlord policies are a special type of property insurance designed specifically for investors and property managers. Fire policies are sometimes used as an alternative to landlord policies.

Because our intention is to do a lease-option, a Landlord policy for a property is generally the most appropriate. Since our goal is to maximize cash flow while protecting the property from catastrophic loss, we prefer a higher deductible of $1,000.

While taking a $1,000 deductible hit for an insurance claim would be inconvenient and a minor financial setback, it would not be considered a major financial loss for the investment.

We do not claim to be experts in property insurance. The insurance industry continues to change and evolve. However, we have dealt with our fair share of administrative issues in regards to property insurance. We largely rely on our insurance agent to keep us updated on the latest insurance trends, and to provide us sufficient coverage with the most economical premiums possible.

It is important to realize that property insurance, Landlord or Fire policies, generally do not cover any personal contents within the property. Landlord policies generally provide protection only for structural damages and liability protection.

Renters' Insurance

Because we are already discussing property insurance, I would like to add a short comment on renter's insurance. Renter's insurance is a policy tenants should buy to protect their own personal contents. It is not part of our responsibilities to buy this as property managers. Our responsibilities on insurance are limited to property insurance, not renters' insurance.

Reviewing the Numbers Again

This chapter largely focuses on the types of properties we recommend you buy. When buying property, we always keep the selling end in mind.

In Chapter 2, we presented sample transactions for you to view and study. I have again included the two examples here for your convenience. I recommend that you review these numbers once again keeping in mind the type of properties we look to purchase.

Using Bank Financing

"BUY"

Fair Market Value:	**$50,000**	**30-year Finance @ 7% interest**	
Purchase Price:	$45,000	Mortgage Pymt:	$266.33
(-) 10% Down:	$ 5,000	Taxes & Insurance:	$ 99.67
= 90% Finance:	$40,000	Total P.I.T.I.:	$366.00

Closing Costs: $ 2,000
(Additional cash)

Our Holding Costs
(2 months)

P.I.T.I.:	$ 732.00
Marketing:	$ 300.00
Total Holding:	$1,032.00

"SELL"

"Owner-Financing" with Lease-Option

Option Price:	$60,000	Tenant's Monthly Pymt:	$ 600.00
(-) Upfront Money:	$ 1,600		
= Refinance Price:	$58,400		

Contract Equity Position:	*$13,400.00*
Total Cash Investment:	*$ 8,032.00*
Net Cash Investment:	*$ 6,432.00*
Net Cash flow:	*$234.00/month*
Annual cash flow:	*$ 2,808.00*
Cash-on-Cash Returns:	***43.6%***

Better returns than savings accounts, certificates of deposits (CDs), mutual funds, and most stocks!

Using Private Financing

"BUY"

Fair Market Value: $50,000

Purchase Price:	$42,500
(-) 0% Down:	$ zero
= 100% Finance:	$42,500

5-Year Loan @ 10% interest

Interest-only Pymt:	$354.17
Taxes & Insurance:	$ 95.83
Total I.T.I.:	$450.00

Closing Costs: $ 450
(Additional cash)

Our Holding Costs
(2 months)

I.T.I.:	$ 900.00
Marketing:	$ 300.00
Total Holding:	$1,200.00

"SELL"

"Owner-Financing" with Lease-Option

Option Price:	$60,000
(-) Upfront Money:	$ 1,600
= Refinance Price:	$58,400

Tenant's Monthly Pymt: $ 600.00

Contract Equity Position:	*$13,400.00*
Total Cash Investment:	*$ 1,650.00*
Net Cash Investment:	*$ 50.00*
Net Cash flow:	*$150.00/month*
Annual cash flow:	*$ 1,800.00*
Cash-on-Cash Returns:	***3,600.0%***

Returns are off the scale with no basis of comparison!

Summary

Identifying and buying the right investment property for a lease-option transaction is part of the homework we do as property managers and investors. Knowing what numbers will work with the lease-option strategy is largely determined by the type of property we buy. We not only look at the cost of the property, we look at how we buy and what type of financing to use. For us, we prefer buying with private financing followed by seller-financing. Conventional financing is the least desirable method of purchase.

Written Exercise – Part 1

Did I truly understand the main points of this chapter? What do I need to review again?

Which ideas in this chapter can I adapt to my market?

Which ideas in this chapter can I start implementing immediately?

Written Exercise – Part 2

Which tasks do I need to do myself? Which tasks do I need to delegate to others?

What team members do I need to contact to assist me in implementing the ideas within this chapter?

What follow-up questions do I need to ask the Author? What additional information do I need to research?

5 Preparing the Property

The Goals of Preparation

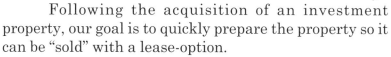

Following the acquisition of an investment property, our goal is to quickly prepare the property so it can be "sold" with a lease-option.

When we prepare the property for a resale with a lease-option, we have the following objectives in mind:

- Maximize the upfront money
- Maximize the monthly payment
- Minimize the repair and maintenance costs
- Minimize the vacancy costs

Most importantly, we seek to balance the money and time being invested vs. what we will receive in return.

Keep in mind the goal is not necessarily to spend NO money. The consequence of trying to spend nothing can be disastrous when well-placed expenses can make a significant difference on the overall salability of a property.

At the same time, the goal is not to do an overhaul or a total renovation of the property either. Why? The likelihood of totally recovering money spent and vacancy costs for a complete renovation is nearly impossible from a cash flow perspective.

We take a balanced approach. Keep in mind what is required in one market may be different in another. Some markets are more demanding than others. Fortunately, we live in a market where tenant expectations are reasonable.

There is no set formula for every property, but there are general guidelines we follow.

Preparation Guidelines

In preparing our properties for resale, we often make minor cosmetic, landscaping, and other relatively inexpensive improvements.

Most of the properties we buy are structurally sound and in livable condition. However, they often require some cosmetic improvements and minor repairs.

As part of our preparation, we visually inspect the property to determine improvements to be made or at least noted prior to putting the property on the market.

Some of the things we look at in our inspection include:

- ***Carpeting and flooring*** – We inspect the carpeting and flooring of every room. We focus on the kitchen floors and the bathroom floors. Many times, we find that the carpet has been worn, damaged, or simply too dirty to clean.
- ***Interior Trash & Debris*** – We inspect the interior of the property for any remaining personal contents, trash, or debris left by the

sellers or the prior tenants. Any remaining debris, contents, or trash will have to be removed.

- ***Interior Walls*** - We inspect the interior walls for damage, markings, and discolorations to the walls or paint.
- ***Plumbing*** – We inspect bathroom and kitchen faucets for any leaks and check to see if toilets flush properly.
- ***Doors & Locks*** – We inspect the doors, locks, and doorframes leading to the exterior. We place a lesser priority with bedroom, bathroom, and interior doors.
- ***Windows*** – We inspect for damaged or broken windows that would expose the interior to the outside weather.
- ***Landscaping*** – We look to see if the lawn needs to be cut or any shrubs or bushes need to be trimmed. We also look to see if there is any debris or trash in the yard area that might diminish the curb appeal of the property.
- ***Environmental units*** – We inspect the heating and air-conditioning units to ensure they are operational.
- ***Appliances*** – We inspect the kitchen appliances (if any) to ensure they are operational.

Although this partial list may look somewhat long on paper, very often by the time we have bought the property, we will have determined 90% of the problem areas that must be dealt with. In fact, we are so accustomed to inspecting and preparing our properties for lease-option, even if we have never seen the property, we can do a property inspection within 10 minutes.

Contrary to popular belief, the point of our inspections is not to necessarily correct every problem we see. The point of the inspections is to get a complete sales assessment of the property.

There are things we do to improve the property, but there are things we do not. It is important to know that we treat potential tenants with intelligence. Most imperfections, either obvious or not, will generally be found out once someone moves in. By doing the inspection ourselves, we become knowledgeable about the property and its imperfections. This way we either correct it or verbally acknowledge it during the sales process.

I would like to add that we occasionally hire professional inspectors when we suspect structural or mechanical problems with the roof, foundation, electrical system, plumbing, and environmental systems.

Utility Service

Once we have done the inspection, we have a good plan of action as to what needs to be done. Before we can hire anyone to begin work, we have to activate electric and water service.

This can be somewhat cumbersome depending which jurisdiction we are working within. Each utility company has different activation requirements. Some we can do with a phone call. Others, we have to do in person. Nevertheless, we activate these services because without electric and water service, it is nearly impossible to prepare the property to our standards.

Standard Improvements

The improvements we do vary from property to property. But there are "universal" improvements we always commit to do for each and every property.

General Housekeeping

We hire a contract housecleaner to come in to spray, clean, and wipe down every surface in the house. This includes windowsills, counter tops, kitchen & bathroom drawers, shelves, windows, ceiling fans, and appliances. Every toilet, sink, and basin is scrubbed. Additionally, every room that has carpeting must be vacuumed.

Those rooms without carpeting, such as the kitchen and bathroom, must be wiped down or mopped. The housecleaner will also remove all the light trash and contents left by the previous owners or tenants.

Our experience has shown the overall impact of a good interior housecleaning significantly improves the entire sales process. Even the most cosmetically-challenged properties are noticeably improved after a good housecleaning.

General Landscaping

We hire a contract yard person to mow our loans, remove leaves, light branches, and sweep the walkway and driveways. He will also remove any trash or debris left in the yard or storage sheds.

We are constantly amazed at how much difference it makes to the overall salability of the property after hiring someone to do some basic landscaping and yard work. Very often, it sets a nice precedent for our tenants to follow.

Similar to a good housecleaner, a good yard person can substantially improve the sales appeal of even the most cosmetically-challenged properties.

Environmental Systems

In our area, people are very sensitive to the functionality of heating and air-conditioning units. The local climate gets hot enough in spring through autumn when air-conditioning is required. Naturally, the summers are the worst and simply unbearable without air-conditioning. There is no disputing that functional air-conditioners are required for any decent housing unit in our area.

On the flip side, the local climate gets cold enough where heating units are required during the winter.

We have occasionally attempted to sell our houses without functional heating and air-conditioning units. Unfortunately, we found out early in our investing careers, there was too much resistance in our market to be able to practically and effectively sell our property without functional heating and air-conditioning units. So, when we discover a problem with the environmental systems, it is nearly a foregone conclusion we will have to either repair or replace the units.

Carpeting & Flooring

We very rarely make improvements to the carpet or flooring beyond simple vacuuming or mopping. The replacement of carpet is far too costly for what we do and often it does not significantly hinder the sales process. Instead of paying for new carpet, we take a more creative and less costly approach. We adjust our upfront monies somewhat lower. And we also give generous credits off the option price to our tenants for taking on the responsibility of replacing the carpet and flooring.

Walls & Paint

Again, a paint job is often far too costly an improvement for what we get in return. Instead of committing to a paint job, we acknowledge it during the sales process and lower our upfront money requirements. In addition, we offer a generous paint credit off the option price to the tenant for taking on the responsibility of painting. In our tenant's mind, they feel paint is an easy improvement for them to make. And so, we let them do it for us.

Appliances

As a general rule, we do not put in appliances such as dishwashers, stoves, or refrigerators. When we purchase an investment property, we prefer appliances to be included with the property. We do our best to negotiate the purchase to include the appliances.

Functional appliances do make the property somewhat easier to sell. Unfortunately, when tenants move out, they sometimes take the appliances with them. The most common appliance that is removed is the refrigerator. If that happens, we don't replace it. Nowadays, we inform tenants we will report them to the police for theft if they remove the appliances.

Remember, we tell our tenants we are in the owner-financing business, not the renovation business or the rental business. By now, you realize in a technical sense, we are in fact in the rental business because the heart of what we do is still tied fundamentally to a lease agreement. But to our tenants, they view us as private lenders. So their expectations of our role in the property are lower than if they perceived us as conventional landlords.

Re-keying the Locks

As tenant turnover occurs with our properties, we inevitably encounter the issue of whether we should re-key the locks or not.

As a general rule, we do not re-key the locks. In general, we have little reason to believe the previous tenant will have malicious intent against the property or us. After all, when they move out, what is the worst the previous tenants can do? Break in to a vacant house? And if they want to vandalize the house, new locks certainly wouldn't stop them from doing so.

However, we strongly advise our tenants to re-key the locks after they move-in for their own piece of mind and security. And when they do so, we will need a copy of the new key for emergency access. We find this generally works well.

Everything Else

As I have said, every house we inspect turns up something different. Sometimes there are very few imperfections outside of the items I have mentioned above. Other times, there are more unusual imperfections and challenges such as termites, plumbing, electrical system, water heater, roofing, property settling, drainage, and so forth. These are dealt with on a case-by-case basis. On the negative side, we have encountered these situations and have been forced to deal with them. On the positive side, we are that much wiser and experienced.

If you want to know more about how to deal with more exotic and unusual challenges, you may want to consider ordering our educational program.

Dealing with Unexpected Problems

When unexpected challenges and problems come up or are discovered during the property preparation period, we note these problems so we can either fix the problem or disclose it to the tenants.

These problems must be acknowledged and they must be disclosed. The reason we want to do this is because it is in our best interests to do so. People who move into our investment property ultimately know more about the ins and outs of our property than we do. The reason for this is because they live in it. They eventually use every feature, electrical outlet, window, door, and appliance. It all gets found out in the end.

The last thing we want to have happen is for our tenants to become upset because they were caught off-guard. When we deal with our tenants, we are upfront to disclose all the imperfections we know of, but because we have never lived in the property, it is impossible for us to know every imperfection.

This explanation is often sufficient for most of our tenants. It shows we are genuine and are attempting to look out for them.

We also have them sign a Property Inspection affidavit to confirm we have given them ample time to properly inspect the property for damage or defects. *(We have provided a sample in the Appendix.)*

Show-Stoppers

As I mentioned, problem areas must be acknowledged. Please note I said **acknowledged**, not improved. We prefer simply acknowledging a problem to the tenant and presenting it to them to respond. Often, finding the right tenant with the right attitude solves the problem. They say, "Oh, I am not worried about it. I can easily fix it." It's all in our approach.

Occasionally, we run into a few situations we call "show-stoppers" to the sales process. Early on, we attempted to sell a house that had either a heating or air-conditioning problem in "as is" condition. Unfortunately, we found we were unable to sell the house even under very favorable terms. We discovered for our area, people would not buy a house with a significant heating or air-conditioning problem. We have learned if we do encounter a heating or air-conditioning problem, our show-stoppers, we have to fix it before it can be sold.

Another "show-stopper" we recently learned about is the issue of termites. As investors, we do not necessarily let minor termite problems dissuade us from buying. We know a pest control specialist can professionally treat it. In fact, after treatment, they even provide certification of treatment and a guarantee, which is acceptable to most established lenders.

However, in our potential tenant's eyes, it can be a scary proposition for them to take on an untreated property. Although they could hire a pest control specialist just as we have, tenants in our area are too fearful of the process. In the end, we've learned if we have any future termite problems, we will probably have to treat it before selling it to a potential tenant.

As you may realize by now, we prepare our property based on the "bang for the buck" as in the case of general housekeeping and landscaping services. We diligently prepare the property to overcome any "show-stoppers" such as air-conditioning & heating units or termite issues, but that's about it. No renovations or appliance replacements.

Taking a Holistic View

In all of this, we take a holistic view of the property. Every investment property is unique through its mix of size, layout, location, overall condition, and general appearance. Aside from the few items I have noted, there are few absolutes in the preparation process.

There have been times we have "shortcut" the process (often unintentionally) where we have bypassed the housekeeping and landscaping process because a potential tenant discovers one of our nicer properties has just become available. If they are emotionally involved and attracted to our property, they often want to secure the property quickly so it is not lost to someone else.

The preparation process often takes no more than one week, sometimes two, depending on the availability of our contract help.

No Major Renovation Projects Wanted

As a reminder, it is important to realize when we buy, we do not seek out major property renovation or rehabilitation projects. It is not currently our line of specialty. Our focus is to continue building an investment portfolio that we manage for our investment partners (and ourselves) who are interested in earning good returns and steady cash flow.

We believe the reason we successfully and consistently perform well is because we do not get pulled into any major or costly renovation projects. It is part of our overall strategy of staying focused.

Although we deal with houses as an investment vehicle, we are in the cash flow and portfolio management business, not in the house-fixing business.

Summary

Preparing the property for a lease-option "resale" is the last step prior to showing the property to potential tenants. We have to balance the practicality and costs of improving the property against the returns we receive. Through field and market experience, we have determined guidelines that seem to work best for us in our area. We follow a property preparation list that guides the inspections and cost-effective improvements we make to produce a profitable resale.

Written Exercise – Part 1

Did I truly understand the main points of this chapter? What do I need to review again?

Which ideas in this chapter can I adapt to my market?

Which ideas in this chapter can I start implementing immediately?

Written Exercise – Part 2

Which tasks do I need to do myself? Which tasks do I need to delegate to others?

What team members do I need to contact to assist me in implementing the ideas within this chapter?

What follow-up questions do I need to ask the Author? What additional information do I need to research?

6 Marketing Properties

Acquiring an investment property is only one part of the equation. An investment property without a paying tenant is a losing proposition. So the next step is to expertly and effectively market our properties to attract applicants.

Many beginning investors believe it is the real estate itself that is valuable. However, without a market base and a tenant to move into the property, the investment property in itself is a non-performing asset.

Only by finding a good tenant who is committed to the lease-option process will we have a performing asset.

Multi-Front Marketing

As a management company, we market simultaneously on four fronts:

- Our Business Name
- The Property

- The Owner-Finance Concept
- Our Market Position & Specialization

It all begins with our business name: OwnerFinanceHomes.com.

Our Business Name

Our true corporate name is different from our day-to-day business name. We actively promote **OwnerFinanceHomes.com** as our business name. It is no coincidence that our business name is the name of our website. Not only is it used for our website; it is the name we use for ourselves in print, audio, and electronic advertising.

Everywhere we can, we like to refer ourselves as "OwnerFinanceHomes.com". The beauty of this is our name is a powerful description of what we do and our specialization, and also drives traffic to our website.

In fact, all our flyers and newspaper advertising includes our website with our property advertisements. The website name, tagged with our phone numbers in the advertisements, sends a powerful message to the tenant community.

No matter what properties we advertise, or whether a prospective applicant is interested in a particular property or not, thousands of people become aware of our business, our specialty, and our ongoing presence in the community at large.

The Property

Marketing at the property front is the most obvious. We talk about the features of the property, its location, monthly rent, and the upfront money required for the property. It is what most people focus on.

However, with every advertisement we run, we always include our business name: **OwnerFinanceHomes.com**.

The Owner-Finance Concept

The owner-finance concept has been around a long time. We certainly didn't invent the concept. However, we have popularized the owner-finance concept in our local area. Because it is so rare to find a house for sale under owner-financing terms in our local area, it works to our advantage to promote the concept further.

The reason for doing this is so when our "owner-financed" properties come available, demand and interest runs very high. We essentially have a built-in market, and people waiting in line for our property.

Again, part of promoting the concept lies within our business name: **OwnerFinanceHomes.com**.

Our Market Position & Specialization

Along with our business name, our slogan is *"The #1 Source of Owner-Financed Homes!"* The second part of this slogan qualifies it *"Serving the Greater Columbus, Georgia & Phenix City, Alabama area!"*

How can we claim this? Very simple.

Based on our research, no one does owner-financing as consistently, as persistently, or as publicly as we do. And we have been doing it for several years. We specialize in what we do. It is a powerful niche we have claimed within our local area, and unless someone challenges our claim and proves otherwise, we have no qualms in promoting ourselves as our slogan says.

While there are others who occasionally advertise owner-financing and sell with lease-options, no one in our area has consistently and persistently marketed this position and specialization as aggressively as we have.

The reason why we know it works is because many of our clients tell us how long they followed our ads and website (often six months or more).

Overall Effect of Marketing

The overall effect of being consistent and persistent in our multiple-front marketing strategy has enabled us to move properties at less than half the time real estate agencies sell their listed property.

Because the investment portfolio we manage continues to grow steadily, the likelihood of experiencing a vacancy becomes greater with each property we add to the mix.

Please keep in mind, we do not go out of our way to create vacancies *(with the exception of new acquisitions. We generally prefer to buy vacant properties or soon-to-be vacant properties from sellers.)*

Ironically, with each vacancy we have, the greater our marketing exposure in the local market. We try to use economies of scale in our advertising and marketing. For example, advertising three vacant properties generally require almost three times more newspaper space than if we had one vacant property to advertise. However, it does not require three times the cost for additional coverage.

During times of multiple vacancies, we create the perception we are a larger firm than we really are. As such, we often gain greater respect and a larger perceived presence with our potential customers when they do call us. Of course, with more diverse types of properties available, we attract a wider audience as well.

For example, if we had an older 3-bedroom/1-bath house in Georgia, a nice 3-bedroom/2-bath house in Alabama, and a 4-bedroom/2-bath house in Georgia, the types of people we attract would vary greatly. Some would prefer to be an Alabama resident; others prefer to be a Georgia resident. Some would have a smaller family; others would have a larger family. Some would prefer a smaller yard, others a larger yard. Some would have pets, others would not. The different permutations of people that would call on our three houses are nearly endless. It is because of these different permutations that exponentially expand our potential customer base.

Owner-Finance vs. Rent-to-Own

The terms "owner-finance" and "rent-to-own" are casual terms we use for the benefit of people outside of our business. We consider them laymen terms, not technical terms. Both terms are used by investors who lease-option their properties.

However, we have discovered there is a substantial difference in the quality of clientele we attract. The differences lie within their mindset, their sense of responsibility, and their ability to provide additional funds for upfront money and a higher monthly payment.

Renters don't like to take responsibility. Potential buyers and owners do.

The term "rent-to-own" tends to attract people who have little or no upfront money and the renter's mentality. In fact, the term itself begins with the word "rent". So the emphasis in most people's mind is to rent.

The term "owner-finance" conveys financing and a way to buy and ultimately own. This is the way we market our company. Owner-financing tends to attract people who have upfront money and the ability to make higher monthly payments. We like this. People who want to buy and own a home understand the term "owner-finance". And if they don't understand the term, we certainly don't want them in our properties.

Website

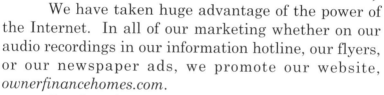

We have taken huge advantage of the power of the Internet. In all of our marketing whether on our audio recordings in our information hotline, our flyers, or our newspaper ads, we promote our website, *ownerfinancehomes.com*.

Our domain name *ownerfinancehomes.com* is self-descriptive. There is very little confusion as to the service we provide, the niche we work within, or how to find us. Once they find our website, they can find our information hotline, our tenant application, our available houses, and our phone numbers. They can even submit their email address to receive email updates of our most recent homes.

In fact, no one in the world can have the same exact Internet domain name as we have. It is unique to us, and we take full advantage of it. While other companies promote their company names, we promote what we do and the owner-financing concept.

When we look at newspaper ads, we sometimes see ads that emulate or mimic our ads. However, they cannot exactly duplicate our presence. As I said earlier, no one else in the world can use the domain *ownerfinancehomes.com*. Like the famous Coca-Cola drink, we are perceived as the "real thing" in our local area whereas our competitors are seen more as dabblers.

Our website continues to be instrumental to our marketing efforts since with each passing month more people obtain access to the Internet. In fact, even low-income people with no computer or Internet connections in their home can access the Internet if they are willing to visit the public library.

Our website initially started out as a credibility-building tool. It has since become an information resource center and a fully legitimate advertising medium. We have pictures, descriptions, addresses, directions, applications, and even maps to our available properties. It helps to alleviate the need for extra staff to mail out literature and field calls.

Signs

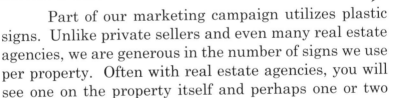

Part of our marketing campaign utilizes plastic signs. Unlike private sellers and even many real estate agencies, we are generous in the number of signs we use per property. Often with real estate agencies, you will see one on the property itself and perhaps one or two more by the main street.

We believe signs are a very inexpensive way to market our properties. So, for each property that is vacant, we use multiple signs. We frequently place two signs on the property itself, and we generously place more signs at all the major entrances into the neighborhood whenever possible.

Occasionally, our signs are removed. It is an unfortunate circumstance when this happens, but we continue to replace them until our property is off the market. Then we are diligent to remove and store them for future use.

Flyers

We post bright, neon-colored information flyers on the front door of all our vacant properties. It provides a snapshot of all the relevant information a potential tenant would want to know including: how much upfront money they need and thc monthly payment. We also provide them with a phone number and our website.

The bright flyers, in themselves, do not attract potential tenants to our properties. But when used in conjunction with our signs, newspaper ads, and our website, the flyers become another piece of our marketing strategy.

What matters most, is the information we give to a potential tenant right then and there. They have the facts in front of them and can immediately assess whether or not this is something they can afford. It's immediate gratification for them.

Information Hotline

We have a dedicated, telephone line connected to an automated answering system that provides information on our properties 24-hours a day, 7-days a week to potential customers and other interested parties.

The answering system is updated periodically to provide the latest information and the availability of our properties. We include a short description, the upfront money required, the monthly payment, the address, and directions to available properties. The idea behind the information hotline is, in addition to our website, it is an information resource for potential customers. For interested parties who aren't Internet users, the information hotline via telephone is an effective means to get information from us 24-hours a day, 7 days a week.

Our marketing is geared to drive initial customer traffic to either the information hotline or our website. The idea is to encourage potential customers to learn as much about our available properties, what we do, and for them to visit the properties.

We do not like nor do we encourage telephone shoppers. We want interested parties to first visit our properties before they call us for information. The number to our information hotline is prominently displayed in our newspaper advertising as well as our website.

Newspaper Advertising

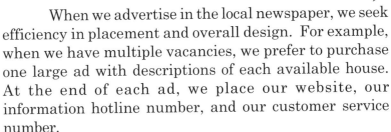

When we advertise in the local newspaper, we seek efficiency in placement and overall design. For example, when we have multiple vacancies, we prefer to purchase one large ad with descriptions of each available house. At the end of each ad, we place our website, our information hotline number, and our customer service number.

As I mentioned earlier, this creates the illusion that we are a larger company than we truly are. If the truth be told, we simply have more vacancies. But the public positively perceives us as having more houses available to choose from. When the vacancies are greater, our exposure and presence becomes greater, and this works out nicely in more ways than one.

Special Situations

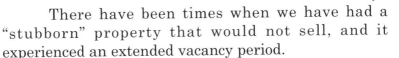

There have been times when we have had a "stubborn" property that would not sell, and it experienced an extended vacancy period.

Yes, I must admit, properties with an extended vacancy period can be an annoyance. After a certain point, the goal is to simply stop the financial bleeding.

Along with re-evaluating what we're offering in terms of upfront money needed and monthly payment requirements, another marketing strategy to draw more interest to the property is by offering a gift item as an incentive. This can include a new TV, microwave oven, or a DVD player. We find drawing attention to a property with a gift item helps further stimulate interest in the property.

Undersell and Overdeliver

One of the pitfalls we have encountered in marketing our houses comes when we oversell or overstate the benefits and features of the property. Any time we have done this, it has resulted in an extended vacancy period.

Why? If we oversell and get people excited enough to visit the property, they are ultimately disappointed when they realize we overstated the benefits and features. This letdown can be detrimental to the overall selling process as well as our reputation as a company. We never want to oversell but we do state selling features in a positive way.

Nowadays, we actually talk about the defects, the work the property needs, or how the property needs paint, carpet, and TLC ("tender loving care"). This reverse-selling approach works for us because when a potential tenant visits the property, they find the property is in better shape than we described it. This creates a feeling of relief and encouragement for them.

When we take this approach, we often hear them say, "The house isn't that bad." And it makes all the difference in the selling process.

Summary

The importance of a marketing system cannot be understated especially when it comes to making an investment property perform. Most management companies focus on the mechanics of property management. The reality is what truly makes our properties perform is having the skill to market the property to attract the right tenant quickly and effectively.

By simultaneously marketing our business on multiple fronts, we have earned the lead position for our specialty in our local area.

Written Exercise – Part 1

Did I truly understand the main points of this chapter? What do I need to review again?

Which ideas in this chapter can I adapt to my market?

Which ideas in this chapter can I start implementing immediately?

Written Exercise – Part 2

Which tasks do I need to do myself? Which tasks do I need to delegate to others?

What team members do I need to contact to assist me in implementing the ideas within this chapter?

What follow-up questions do I need to ask the Author? What additional information do I need to research?

7 Finding the Right Tenants

Generating Activity

When the marketing campaign for any given property begins, activity increases on many fronts.

- We receive more calls into our information hotline.
- We receive more hits to our website.
- We receive more phone calls to our customer service number.
- There are more visitors and drive-bys at the property.

This activity comes from people interested in both our property and the owner-financing program.

Have Tenants Visit the Property

While all this activity occurs, the goal is to guide interested parties into viewing our properties on our website and then personally visit the property, respectively. The goal is for them to be as informed as possible about the property without our taking the time to personally meet them. If we had to meet each and every person interested in looking at our properties, we would not be able to get anything else done. And even if we have more time, it is simply not a good use of our time to show our properties to individual parties. It is much easier for them to go visit the property on their own.

The Application Process

Once a prospective tenant visits the property and remains interested, we take them through our application process, which is very simple. We have them go to our website, print out our online application, and FAX it in. Alternatively, they can mail the application in or personally deliver the application to The UPS Store, our mail receiving service.

With people who do not have computers or Internet access, we suggest they go to the public library and use the Internet terminal there to print out the application. We are grateful to our public library system for providing this service to the general public as it surely helps our business.

As the applicant prepares to submit their application to us, we begin qualifying the tenant.

Qualifying the Tenant

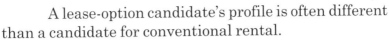

A lease-option candidate's profile is often different than a candidate for conventional rental.

As we market the property, the person who wants "owner-financing" is essentially looking for an alternative way of buying a house and bypassing conventional lending channels. Why? They believe their credit is not strong enough to qualify for a conventional loan. Or they may not have sufficient funds for a larger down payment. Lease-option transactions often require less money upfront.

Another characteristic about our prospective tenants is they are fearful of bankers and lenders and feel more comfortable with a less regimented process.

Last but not least, they are uncertain whether or not they want to fully commit to a house. With a lease-option transaction, they are allowed to "try it out" to see if they truly want the house long-term. Of course, if they do not want the house, they do not receive any of their upfront money back or any of the monthly payments already made. This is the risk they take and we fully inform them of this.

Why is this important information for us to know? It is important to know the typical mindset of our market before they even apply. This alleviates added stress on our part; we have no illusions our candidates will come in having a strong credit background or large amounts of cash for a down payment. Although surprisingly, we have had a few cases where having a good amount of upfront money was not an issue. They simply had little or no credit.

Things to Look At

Although we look at various aspects of an applicant's application, there are three areas we concentrate on:

- Do they comfortably have all the upfront money?
- Are they gainfully employed?
- What is their tenant history like?

It is imperative that we verify the employment of each applicant. We look at the overall household income to ensure they can support the house payments, and we assess and verify their tenant history.

We are careful to follow federal housing laws and not engage in discrimination. However, with all our applicants, we look for their "story".

- Where did they come from?
- Why are they here?
- Why are they moving?
- Why do they want the house?
- How suitable is the house for their financial and personal situation?
- What is their level of desire to buy a house?
- How respectful are they of landlords?
- Do they act suspicious at any level?

These and other questions arise when we interview our applicants.

No Quick Move-Ins Allowed

Occasionally, we encounter people who are in an extreme hurry to move into one of our properties and may not have all the funds to do so. They are immediately suspect for two reasons. We generally do not allow applicants to do "overnight" lease-options even if we are able to. We prefer applicants who have thought carefully through the process and transaction they are entering. Not those who will flake out because there is a two-day delay. Additionally, we want time to verify the statements on their application — especially their employment and tenant history.

Speaking from experience, people who must move quickly are running away from some kind of negative situation. If they are trying to leave their previous landlord quickly, we will not be party to that. By not accepting a fast move-in, it discourages "landlord runners" to come into our properties. Although, other landlords are our competitors, we still believe if an incoming tenant treats their previous landlord badly by leaving on bad terms, they will probably do the same with us.

Ideally, good lease-option candidates have never bought a house and want "their big chance" to buy a house. They have the upfront money and can make the monthly payments. They have verifiable employment, income, and a good tenant history. They have a responsible attitude and are willing to create "sweat equity" by making improvements to the property and generally have pride in where they live. This is our ideal tenant.

Match the Applicant to the Property

As I have said before, each property is unique in its own way. It almost goes without saying, the way we qualify someone for a more cosmetically-challenged property is not the same as the way we qualify someone for a nicer, more established property.

For example, our more cosmetically-challenged properties command lower upfront money and a lower monthly payment than nicer, more established properties. When we qualify an applicant for our lower-end properties, we look more closely at their fix-up ability and willingness to do work to improve the property. On a nicer, more established property, we pay closer attention to a candidate's financial strength and tenant history.

No matter which house, we always listen to the applicant's story to ensure the property matches the applicant. Just because they have the money does not automatically give them approval. Just like conventional landlording, we will not simply accept anyone even if they can afford the security deposit and monthly payment.

Let Applicants Sort Themselves Out

Because we take a portfolio view of how we manage properties, we also look at our vacancy level. If vacancy levels are high, we become a bit more lenient in the qualifying process. If our vacancy levels are low, we tend to be more stringent. Regardless of our vacancy levels, we will not knowingly accept tenants with a criminal record, a bad tenant history, or no source of verifiable income.

Often we let applicants qualify or disqualify themselves by letting them know upfront our expectations and intentions to verify their background. Often, the situation sorts itself out.

For example, if we suspect an applicant is providing us questionable information on their application, we will insist on verifying the information. Either they will be cooperative or they will not. If they are not cooperative and back out, it is a good sign they were not dealing truthfully with us. In these cases, the situation sorted itself out and worked out for the best.

It is important to realize when we qualify applicants, our intention is to try to accommodate their personal and financial situation. After all, we are in the business of serving others while maximizing occupancy of our properties. And we tell them so. However, as we try to accommodate them, we also evaluate the risk we must take to do so. If the risk is too high, we are forced to disqualify them and look for another candidate.

Sometimes, it is simply better to have a vacancy than to take on a bad tenant. And while that was a short statement, it is probably the most important piece of advice I can give to any investor or property manager looking for a tenant to live in one of their investment properties.

Summary

Finding the right tenant for our properties is a combination of science and art. Generically speaking, we know the type of clientele we serve. As such, we know how to direct them during their initial levels of interest. We simply have them learn as much as possible about our properties through our information hotline and our website. Then we have them visit the property.

However, our experience has shown there is still a good amount of diversity we encounter once we get to the application process. Even by our more lenient standards, we must still qualify the tenant. If and when they meet our qualification standards, we then guide them to the closing process.

Written Exercise – Part 1

Did I truly understand the main points of this chapter? What do I need to review again?

Which ideas in this chapter can I adapt to my market?

Which ideas in this chapter can I start implementing immediately?

Written Exercise – Part 2

Which tasks do I need to do myself? Which tasks do I need to delegate to others?

What team members do I need to contact to assist me in implementing the ideas within this chapter?

What follow-up questions do I need to ask the Author? What additional information do I need to research?

8 Closing the Lease-Option Transaction

Definition of a Closing

A "closing" is a term used in the real estate industry meaning "coming to an agreement and signing of the contracts by all parties."

The closing of a lease-option contract with a tenant is far simpler than a closing of any property purchase with a conventional mortgage. There is considerably less paperwork and fewer legal issues to deal with because title is not being transferred.

Because the closing of a lease-option transaction with our tenants does not require a notary or third-party witness, the location is flexible.

Schedule the Closing

When we set up appointments to close with our applicants, we generally do it in the late afternoon unless otherwise requested. The reasons for this are many.

First, we almost always insist on a confirmation call prior to the closing. Because we often meet outside of our office, we do not want to risk a no-show. It's a waste of our time and energy. Rarely does it happen, but sometimes someone will get held up or have changed their minds without informing us.

Most times, our applicants have to work during the day so it is much easier to meet after they get off work. Another good point is there are not as many time constraints towards the end of the day, so this allows for a more leisurely closing.

An afternoon closing minimizes disruption and rhythm of our workday. It is much easier for us to prepare for the closing; all documentation can be gathered in the morning/early afternoon and be ready for a late afternoon meeting since there is no point in preparing contracts until the confirmation call is completed.

Once we schedule the closing by phone, we ask our applicants to bring originals and photocopies of:

- Proper identification
- Social Security card
- Certified funds
  (Money order or Cashier's check)
- Proof of income

Where We Close

We never set up a closing at the property because it is generally uncomfortable and we need a convenient place to comfortably sit and discuss the lease-option contracts.

Although we have access to standard offices, we often do our closings at local fast-food restaurants. Why? These restaurants are highly visible, conveniently located, and easy to find. It is also a non-threatening, friendly environment.

A fast-food restaurant allows for our applicants to relax and get a snack or beverage prior to the closing. Generally, it is an upbeat atmosphere that reduces some of the tension and nervousness some of our applicants experience. For many of our applicants, lease-optioning a property is one of the largest transactions they have ever made. No somber mood of "signing your life away" or anything of that sort. We want it to be a happy occasion for them.

We find the casual atmosphere works in our favor and is less intimidating for our applicants.

At the time of closing, we are careful to take the time to converse with each applicant to ensure they fully understand the transaction they are entering. We also reconfirm their intentions to buy and fully take responsibility for the property. We allow them to ask questions or discuss any issue relating to the house.

The whole point of this conversational period is to put them at ease; to allow them "breathing room" to make sure they want to complete this transaction. It also allows us the opportunity to stop the closing if new information reveals they are unqualified to close the transaction.

Generally, taking the time for this conversational period makes the contract review and signing a much smoother process.

Contract Review

After the preliminary conversations, we move into the contract review stage. We make it a practice to never engage in "sign and run". Although we have many people who would prefer to simply take the keys and be on their way, we do not allow it. We take our time to do a firm closing to make sure they understand their responsibilities and the details of the lease-option transaction.

Often, we meet new applicants personally for the first time at the closing because so much of the initial communication has been done by phone.

Evaluating Applicants During Closing

While we want our applicants to be at ease during the closing process, we also want to emphasize to them the rules they must follow. Remember, at any time during the closing process, we reserve the right to change our minds and not complete the transaction. How they respond to us initially will be an indication of how they will respond to us later as tenants.

If they are inattentive, disruptive, disrespectful, or simply ignorant of the major points up to this point, this is a red flag. Fortunately, this almost never occurs. For the most part, our new tenants are polite, respectful, and eager to complete the closing.

Immediately prior to reviewing the contracts, we verify whether they have brought originals and photocopies of items we requested earlier:

- Proper identification
- Social Security card

- Certified funds
  (Money order or Cashier's check)
- Proof of income

Missing any of these will complicate the closing process. Getting photocopies of these documents are important. If they did not bring them as requested, we need to find a way to get them in a timely manner.

The Rhythm of Closing

Because we have done many closings, there is a certain rhythm we have adopted. We take the same basic approach and presentation.

The sophistication level of the applicants determines how deeply we get into explaining the contracts. As a general rule, we take a middle-of-the-road approach. We do not read to them word-for-word any of the contracts. However, we do not simply allow them to sign a document without some kind of review. What we do is verbally highlight major points and clauses on every page.

As we review the major clauses within each document, we move at a good pace so we don't bore the tenants. Remember, these are legal-binding documents. As such, this is not necessarily exciting to our applicants, so we try to present it in a positive, upbeat fashion and solicit affirmations from them that they understand us.

Contracts & Forms

Early in our investing careers, the contracts and forms we used was a conglomeration of documents developed by other attorneys and investors. We picked, chose, and adapted the portions we liked and discarded the others. As time has progressed, our contracts and forms have evolved into a package we call our own. It is highly effective and useful as a *baseline set* to anyone who wants to execute lease-option transactions like we do.

I would like to point out there are many ways to implement a lease-option transaction. There is no one right way. The contracts and forms we use is specifically customized for our needs, circumstances, and legal environment. As we gain experience and encounter new circumstances or unusual properties, we modify our baseline contracts and forms accordingly. The actual documents within our contracts and forms package vary. We have documents that are broad enough to be used in any part of the U.S. There are other documents we have specific to a property or the area the property is in.

If you would like to purchase our Contracts and Forms package to use as your baseline, you can order it from our website at *www.turnkeyinvesting.com*.

Signing the Contracts

Once the contract review is over, we have our new tenants sign two sets of originals. One set is for them to keep; one set is for our office files. We keep the photocopies of their identification, Social Security cards, proof of income, and we fully accept the certified funds they bring.

At this point, we give them their keys and a copy of their contracts. We also direct them to transfer the electric and water utilities into their names and remind them of their next payment due date.

Overall, the entire closing from beginning to end lasts 30 to 45 minutes, depending on how many questions or concerns our new tenants may have.

Contracts to Close

The documents we use to close our lease-options occasionally deviate, but this list outlines most of our baseline documents.

- Lease-Option Funds Distribution Receipt
- Lease Agreement
- Option Agreement
- Security Deposit Agreement
- Lease-Option Disclosure Statement
- Appliance Inventory
- Administration Fee Agreement
- Property Inspection Agreement

Disconnect Utility Service

Following the closing, we immediately arrange for both electric and water service to be discontinued. (Utilities were initially turned on to prepare the property for resale.) We have, on occasion, allowed utility service to remain on for a few extra days during move in. It was to allow them time to transfer service without interruption out of convenience to our new tenants. Unfortunately, we found some tenants abused this privilege and were intentionally slow in transferring service. As a result, we no longer allow this privilege and inform our new tenants they should expect interruption of utility service.

Summary

Successfully closing a lease-option transaction is the culmination of many careful and planned steps. If done correctly, an investment property becomes a performing asset.

A successful closing is a happy occasion for our new tenants. The home they have sought to purchase through an owner-financing program becomes a reality when the transaction is completed. Our tenants go away knowing what their responsibilities are. If all goes well, our tenants continue to be happy with the home, and we are happy to receive their payments regularly each and every month.

Written Exercise – Part 1

Did I truly understand the main points of this chapter? What do I need to review again?

Which ideas in this chapter can I adapt to my market?

Which ideas in this chapter can I start implementing immediately?

Written Exercise – Part 2

Which tasks do I need to do myself? Which tasks do I need to delegate to others?

What team members do I need to contact to assist me in implementing the ideas within this chapter?

What follow-up questions do I need to ask the Author? What additional information do I need to research?

9 Dealing with Defaults & Non-Payment

As with conventional rentals, tenants in a lease-option transaction can become slow payers or non-payers. If non-payment occurs, I refer it to as a **default**. In essence, a default results in the financial non-performance of the investment we have set up.

Many times there are warning signs leading up to a default. Sometimes, tenants will inform us that they will be late. Other times, it occurs suddenly and without any warning. Regardless of how it occurs, we must quickly move to resolve the situation.

A good payer can suddenly become a non-payer; this puts us in a situation where we need to make a decision. Do we immediately take steps to have them leave the property or do we give them additional time to perform?

Course of Action is Not Always Clear

As I look back at all the various default situations we have encountered, there are still many times when I must pause before deciding on a course of action. On paper, it is easy to have a blanket policy to either take steps to have someone evicted immediately or to automatically give them additional time. But the bottom line is since this is a very people-oriented business, we must look at each situation one at a time.

As an investor and property manager, it is my job to ensure the investment performs. My priorities are crystal clear; *I never treat my lease-option business and investment portfolio as a charity or social service.* I am engaged in this business to earn a profit and a good return for my investors and myself. Period. In fact, *I have a fiduciary responsibility to first take care of the investor.* If the greater good is served by removing the existing tenant, then we don't hesitate to take the steps to do so.

However, I also make sure I make reasonable efforts to allow the tenant to perform from both a customer service and legal point of view. Although we have been to eviction court many times and have escalated eviction accounts to collection accounts, it is something we do as a last measure when negotiations have failed.

The Big Picture

When non-payment occurs, it is imperative to remember the "big picture." Our achievement goals must be foremost in our minds. Why? Because as property managers, sometimes we can get drawn into the human drama that inevitably comes from our tenants and their problems.

On a lower level, we are trying to get paid. On a higher level, we want our investment property to perform.

In the absence of payment, we must regain legal possession of the property quickly. This is essential. Without legal possession, a non-performing property will continue to stay non-performing.

With legal possession, we can then prepare the property for resale to make it a performing asset.

Working with the Tenant

If a tenant is experiencing a temporary setback or financial hardship, and they express a desire to get back on track, we generally ask for a goodwill gesture. That goodwill gesture is partial payment within the first 10 days of default. If the tenant can provide at least 50% of what they owe during the first 15 days of default, we will generally accept the money, knowing there is a still a slight risk they will not pay the remaining amount owed. *I would like to caution that this is a very loose guideline*; it can vary from property to property and tenant to tenant. We are under no obligation to take partial payments, but we reserve the right to do so on our terms.

Some people might cringe at this suggestion; most clerks of the court system and others in the legal profession say do NOT take partial payments because you will endanger your right to evict for that month. And yes, they are correct.

However, these people are not investors; they do not know what it is like to be responsible for the financial performance of a given investment property. The risk of holding real estate as a cash flow investment is the monthly obligation to the lender who financed the purchase of the investment property in the first place.

Taking Financial Responsibility

When default occurs and we don't receive any monies from a tenant that month, we actually LOSE money because of the outgoing payment. This is why most beginning investors cannot cope with a default situation; they are not emotionally, mentally, or financially equipped to carry vacancies or unexpected expenses if and when it occurs.

This is also why few property management companies do what we do. Most conventional property management companies put this financial burden entirely on the owner of the property. This is one reason why so many owners of rental property become dismayed with the performance of their investment. It's because their property managers are not investors. The property owners pay for their property manager's inefficiency, lack of business and investing knowledge.

Many property managers only know how to prevent risk to themselves and send bills to the property owners. They forget their job it to not only manage and lease the property, but their long-term goal should be to help make investment properties perform well financially for the property owners.

How We Work with Tenants

The reason I will accept 50% (or more) of the lease payment is because those monies will cover at least 60%-75% of the money that has already been paid out for the underlying mortgage. *(Remember, we must fulfill our monthly obligations to our lenders and investment partners regardless of our tenant's performance.)*

Before accepting a partial payment, we will verbally assess the tenant's intentions. If the tenant does not show remorse, concern, or any sign of personal responsibility, then we do not accept partial payments and we quickly move to the eviction process. If we feel the tenant experienced a temporary setback but can still recover, we will work with them.

Maintaining Cash Reserves

Normally, we carry sufficient cash reserves in our holding account to ensure all mortgage payments are made for any given month, regardless of the status of our tenant's payments. This cash reserve can fluctuate up and down depending on our vacancy level or default rate. How we keep our cash reserves up (and also the overall investment performance) is by encouraging continued payments, even if it is a partial payment.

For example, let's suppose we have an investment property with a $500 monthly payment which has already been paid out; our tenant's monthly obligation is $700. If we were to follow the advice of "no partial payments", we would simply be out $500 for the month, and we'd have to immediately pay and file for eviction.

Although the actual court process itself is generally resolved within 2 to 3 weeks depending on the time of month we file, the actual time we will get legal possession of the investment property will be in 30-45 days. This is because we must factor in setting an appointment with the Marshal or Sheriff's Office to reclaim the property.

As you can see, the additional 30-45 days on top of the first 5-7 days lost to negotiate an acceptable remedy with the tenant really translates to nearly two months of non-performance.

You may be asking yourself, "What is the difference of taking partial payment only to evict them later?"

The difference largely involves the intangible issue of ***time***. Remember, when we took the partial payment within 10 days, it covered at least half of the month's income for that investment. We, in effect, "bought" ourselves two weeks at "full pay" to better assess the slow-pay situation.

Keep the End Goals in Mind

As I have continuously emphasized throughout this book, we are both investors and property managers. The goal is to have our investments perform well. In order for this to happen, we must find the right people to lease-option our investment properties. When problems arise, we must give ourselves the maximum opportunity to remedy a non-performing situation. By taking partial payment, we at least buy ourselves more time to make a better-informed decision.

The extra time allows us to inspect the property, gather more information, further assess the tenant's intentions, explore our collection options, and plan for the next phase.

Watch Tenants Carefully

Assuming the tenants have shown a sense of distress, good intentions, and reassurances for full payment by the third week of the month, we allow them the opportunity to make good on their promise. I am happy to say with few exceptions, partial payment tenants have very rarely forced us into a court situation.

Because our tenants know we are keeping a watchful eye, they either pay us in full before the end of the month, or they come to the conclusion they must move out. If they pay us in full, the investment continues to perform. If they decide to move out on their own accord by the end of the month and sign a property release, we lose very little time compared to going through the court system. Yes, it is inconvenient to get a property back despite efforts to help the tenant out. But it is far more preferable than fighting to get a property back through the court system.

In our experience, there is a clear difference between non-payers and slow payers. Non-payers are those who either need to be evicted or those who will eventually abandon a property. Slow payers are people who are habitually late but ultimately do pay. While I never go out of my way to encourage late fees, I do enforce them. And those late fees make up for the "inconvenience" of waiting the extra one to three weeks.

Types of Landlords

Early in my investment career, I was confident I wouldn't allow myself to fall into the trap of letting tenants ride me out month after month, making me chase rent. Unfortunately many new investors and property managers fall into this category.

Based upon my experience and knowledge of conventional landlording, there are two bad ways to handle tenants: being socialistic or dictatorial landlords.

Socialistic Landlords

First is the *socialistic landlord.* He is the person who feels sorry for his tenants and listens to all their excuses. In doing so, this landlord has tenants who are never current on their payments; he must chase the rent each and every month. He needs the money so bad he will go and pick it up from the tenant.

Basically, he calls month after month and drives over to pick it up. This wastes lots of time and energy. For the most part, this type of landlord also hates evictions because he doesn't have the stomach for it. He feels like he is throwing a family to the streets. The reality is this type of landlord is ignorant. Few tenants will let themselves simply live in the streets. Almost everyone has somewhere to go and live temporarily in times of need. This landlord pays for the privilege to house sorry tenants.

The reality of the situation is most tenants are intelligent enough to know that professional management companies rarely put up with such nonsense. Usually it's the private landlord who individually manages his properties that puts himself through this. Most professional management companies realize they'd be out of business if they practiced this type of nonsense month after month. In fact, the property owners that hired them would probably fire them. Very little rent comes in with a socialistic attitude.

Tenants are smart enough to keep themselves off the streets, despite what these socialistic landlords think. While these problem tenants are busy abusing the existing landlord, they are saving their money to move into their next residence.

Dictatorial Landlords

The other type of landlord is the *dictatorial landlord.* It is often a professional management company that is so efficient and sticklers for minute details that their policies actually run off good paying tenants. It is actually a disadvantage for tenants to stay longer in their properties.

Unfortunately, how I know this is from first-hand experience having been a tenant myself. Having never been late and always rules-abiding, it was very upsetting to know there was very little consideration for being a good tenant. While they were strict, the management never instilled any loyalty within me because of their ruthless policies.

It is generally easy to tell what companies they are. All you have to do is look to the property managers.

If the property managers have little authority of their own and continually claim that all tenants are supposed to be treated the same regardless of their account standing, then someone "upstairs" is missing the point.

Good paying tenants should get more consideration than slow or non-paying ones. Even good payers make the occasional mistake. There is room for some degree of consideration.

We have to be careful that our policies encourage continued loyalty and reward timely payments, not run off our good-paying ones.

Sign and Leave

In cases of extreme slow payment or non-payment by tenants, we practice a technique called "Sign and Leave".

"Sign and Leave" is an extremely effective alternative to the time-consuming and sometimes costly eviction process. By its nature, the eviction process is an adversarial process. Because of this, we choose to AVOID it whenever possible, but it doesn't mean we will not evict. It simply means we do not use it as our first remedy. In fact, the eviction process is one of our last courses of action. We much prefer the "Sign and Leave" process.

A Simple Process

This simple process is an agreement by the tenant to relinquish legal possession of the property in exchange for us not filing for eviction. We, in effect, allow them out of the lease and leave peacefully. Depending on how much they owe us, we will either negotiate a settlement amount, or we may simply let them go. If they have made a partial payment prior to the "Sign and Leave", we generally accept if they leave quickly before the month is over. If they have not made a partial payment, we inform them they still have to pay for one-month's arrearage.

The True Purpose of "Sign and Leave"

On the surface, it sounds like a risky process depending on their promise to pay. Believe it or not, our first priority is *not* to collect rent from them. Our first priority is to have them to agree to move out and release legal possession of the property back to us. They do so by signing a specially prepared document that specifies they agree to relinquish legal possession of the property in exchange for allowing them out of the lease. We also agree not to file for eviction.

Most tenants believe if we do not file for eviction, then they are safe from collection efforts. While this is not true, we let them believe this. After all, if they sign a document releasing legal possession of the property, there would be no point to filing for eviction. They have, in effect, given the property back to us. We get immediate possession legally and bypass the conventional eviction process.

For the most part, most tenants stop paying on a lease-option contract because they have encountered financial challenges, and they can no longer afford it. There is no point in trying to coax payment from them immediately. The easier road is to get them out and take possession of the property. Collections come later.

As I have said many times, my main objective is to ensure performance of each investment property. If the tenant does not pay or is unable to pay, we must encourage the tenant to leave as quickly as possible so we can find a replacement tenant.

Abandonment

Abandonment of property is when the tenant leaves the property without paying and cannot be contacted or found.

Abandonment can be a problematic situation. It is problematic because in the eyes of the law, the tenant is generally considered to have legal possession of the property unless they specifically and willingly relinquish possession by returning the keys, signing a release document, or going through the eviction process.

Verify Abandonment

With abandonment, the question then arises — did the tenant in fact abandon the property? Were there any prior communications either verbal or written that might indicate they wanted to leave the property? Did they have a spotty payment history?

Before we conclude a property has been abandoned, we do a property inspection to see if it looks occupied. If there are personal contents, how much is in the property? Were the utilities turned off? What is the general condition of the property? Is it relatively orderly and neat or does it look abandoned?

In all cases, if there is non-payment, landlords are allowed to file for eviction if reasonable efforts have been made to contact the tenant. The eviction process is the surefire remedy to non-payment and a suspected abandonment of property. But as you will learn, we have developed a more cost-effective and timely alternative of dealing with abandoned property.

Dealing with Abandonment

We have rarely experienced abandonment of property by our tenants. When we have, we have generally taken the conservative but more time-consuming approach of filing for eviction. In this way, there is little or no grounds to contest our claim of legal possession of the property.

However, as we have learned from developing the Sign and Leave procedure, we have also developed an alternative procedure to deal with abandoned properties. Again, I would like to say it is not a foolproof way to protect ourselves, but it can offer some level of protection if we choose to bypass the eviction process.

Again, how we deal with abandoned properties is done on a case-by-case basis based on the appearance of the property and history of the tenant.

If we feel certain that a tenant has truly abandoned the property, and upon inspection, the property appears abandoned and we feel that no one will likely contest it, we would put together an affidavit detailing the circumstances. Additionally, we would take photos to document the condition of the property prior to our reclaiming the property.

I would like to re-emphasize we will only bypass the eviction process if we feel very certain legal possession will not be challenged, the property clearly looks abandoned, and believe the tenant will never come back.

Evictions

If you recall, the lease-option transaction is fundamentally based on Landlord-Tenant laws. This, of course, is by design. It allows for protection of the property owner, i.e. the investor. Landlord-Tenant laws in my area are well established and considered a standard and affordable legal process.

The remedy of last resort for most landlords is the eviction process.

Early on, as I built my investment portfolio, I frequently used the eviction process if the tenant would not move out willingly. Even if they did move out prior to eviction, I neither got paid, nor did I formally get possession of the property. The only way I could formally get possession of the property (and have it legally recognized) was to go through the entire eviction process. Through experience, I have learned to selectively use the Sign and Leave procedure or the Abandonment procedure as necessary.

While the "Sign and Leave" process may not be as ironclad as the eviction process in reclaiming legal possession, the signed release we receive from the tenant is a compelling piece of evidence if it is ever contested.

Because we operate in multiple counties in Georgia and Alabama, the actual and specific procedures for eviction vary somewhat in each jurisdiction.

Types of Evictions

Fundamentally, there are two types of evictions. First is the eviction to get legal possession (sometimes called a dispossessory warrant). Next is the eviction where you want both legal possession and a formal judgment. A judgment, in simple terms, is the debt owed to a plaintiff as agreed upon by a judge of the court.

There are benefits to each type of eviction. In the first case, you get legal possession, and it does not require the tenant to be served. So, if the tenant is hiding or otherwise unavailable, it does not impede the eviction process. The notice from the court is posted on the front door of the property and whether the tenant actually gets notice or not is unimportant. What is important is that some officer of the court system delivers the notice to the property.

If the tenant fails to respond to the notice or show up to court, the landlord wins by default with no judgment. A dispossessory warrant is issued. After this occurs, an appointment can be made relatively quickly with the Sheriff or Marshal's office to get final possession.

Judgments

In an eviction where we wish to obtain legal possession and a judgment, the tenant must be served with court papers. We like to have papers served at their workplace if possible.

If the tenant is in hiding or otherwise unavailable to receive court papers, it can be a hindrance to the eviction process. However, if we are patient and allow the process to work for us, it can pay off later. Winning a judgment paves the way for follow up collection efforts such as garnishment of wages, money from bank accounts, lien on real property, and levy of personal property.

The detailed discussions of these additional remedies are beyond the scope of the eviction process and this book. I recommend contacting an attorney or your local courthouse if you wish to learn more about them.

Each Eviction is Different

We have executed both types of evictions. How we choose one over the other is done on a case-by-case basis. The biggest deciding factor is: getting the tenants served in a timely manner. There is a limit to how many times an officer of the court will attempt to serve a tenant. Another large factor is whether or not the tenants are working in well-established jobs with reputable employers. If they are, we have a strong possibility of successfully garnishing their wages or salaries.

I would like to emphasize the necessity of our filing for evictions have significantly dropped due to the experience we have gained in recent years. Our emphasis continues to be finding alternative remedies for non-payment and other default situations.

After the Eviction

Once the tenants have been evicted, we have won the case in the court's view. However, when an eviction occurs, there is often an outstanding debt owed to us. It goes without saying, it is often difficult to collect on these debts. Why? Many of the tenants become "runners"; they run and hide like roaches in the night.

Fortunately, as investors, we factor such losses in terms of non-payment and vacancies. Despite this, a tenant's outstanding debt is something we are not prepared to walk away from or entirely write off.

Garnishment

The next step we sometimes take is the garnishment of wages to collect outstanding debts due. One of the reasons we check for steady employment at the start of a Landlord-Tenant relationship is so we have information in case we need to garnish wages through the court system. In fact, we have had good success in doing so. It is certainly well worth the effort, especially when it is successful.

We have also been able to garnish a bank account, which seizes their funds. It is quite disruptive to an ex-tenant, but it does result in getting our monies.

Collection Agency

Unfortunately with the tenants who subsequently leave us with a debt, we find it is very difficult (but not surprising) to collect.

In these situations, we utilize the services of a collection agency. Despite limited success, our philosophy is to continue to collect a portion of the debt owed to us rather than totally write off the debt. The collection agency expends the time and energy to continue the collection effort freeing us to refocus on finding new tenants.

Any monies we receive as a result of the collection agency's efforts are clearly a bonus (which we split with them). More importantly, it sends a strong message to every tenant that improperly leaves our lease-option agreement will have negative consequences to their credit, credit history, and payment record.

On a philosophical note, there are simply too many deadbeats today. Part of the problem is because some landlords are simply too unprofessional, too incompetent, or too lazy to follow up. Even if they do not need the money, letting deadbeat tenants get away without recourse only reinforces the message they can do it to others. We must do our part to prevent that from happening to others.

Summary

Defaults and non-payments will inevitably occur within any investment property portfolio. How well it is handled will often determine the long-term performance of the investment property.

Quite frankly, it is this stage of handling defaults and non-payments that often scares away beginning investors from managing their own properties. In this case it might be best for a beginning investor to work with a management team that has the skill and disposition to promptly handle and resolve the situation.

Written Exercise – Part 1

Did I truly understand the main points of this chapter? What do I need to review again?

Which ideas in this chapter can I adapt to my market?

Which ideas in this chapter can I start implementing immediately?

Written Exercise – Part 2

Which tasks do I need to do myself? Which tasks do I need to delegate to others?

What team members do I need to contact to assist me in implementing the ideas within this chapter?

What follow-up questions do I need to ask the Author? What additional information do I need to research?

10 Administration

Managing a portfolio of investment properties requires a team of advisors we call upon for their professional knowledge and expertise.

As a Management Team, Wes and I ultimately have responsibility for the bottom line and must produce good results for our investment partners. We have fiduciary responsibilities to the city, the county, our tenants, lenders, and investment partners on a daily, weekly, monthly and yearly basis.

Although we consider ourselves to be a smaller business, the scope and people we impact become greater with each new property we acquire. We take our responsibilities very seriously. In order to accomplish our goals, we place a high priority on continually improving and growing our tenant management system and administrative policies.

Tenant Management

We set some strict guidelines for our tenants to remember. This is part of our ongoing tenant management to ensure our tenants continue to meet their financial obligations to us. If they don't, they clearly understand we will pursue legal action against them. In essence, they receive positive reinforcement for following our rules, and plenty of negative reinforcement when they don't.

Our Tenants are Almost Never Right

Many businesses have a written or unwritten mantra they live by that says, "The customer is always right."

What we have learned is that.... our tenants are almost *never* right. The reason why we know this is because we hear all kinds of stories from tenants on how things "should be done" and why it should be "this way or that way" especially when they have difficulties making their monthly payments.

Fortunately, we have written contracts and agreements that are very clear. It outlines their responsibilities as a tenant and what our expectations are from the very beginning. So when they bring up an issue, we are respectful to listen and consider their comments and requests. Very often, they are simply off-base. We must be firm and deny their requests.

Having managed our properties for years, I now say....

> **"We are in a business where the customer is almost never right."**

Tenant Rules and Guidelines

The rules we tell our tenants to follow are:

- Take Ownership Responsibility
- Pay All Utility Bills
- Maintain the Property
- Make & Deliver Payments on Time
- If They Must Move, Arrange to Leave on Good Terms

Take Ownership Responsibility

The whole point of our providing owner-financing is for tenants to learn to take responsibility over their housing situation. Buying and owning a house requires more responsibility than renting a place. We tell them and remind them so. Unfortunately, some of our tenants don't learn this lesson and eventually have to move on for one reason or another.

Pay All Utility Bills

I realize this seems a bit basic, but sometimes it bears repeating with our tenants.

Maintain the Property

Generally, we expect that most tenants who are buying their home will take proper care of the property. Fortunately, most of our tenants do. Occasionally, we have to remind a tenant they should start acting like a homeowner and keep the property in good repair and maintenance.

Again, this is covered when we do a closing but we remind them periodically as circumstances permit. This generally occurs when we do spot inspections on the property.

Make & Deliver Payments on Time

Again, this is very basic, but with some tenants this is a challenge. They sometimes push the edge on paying on time. We almost never encounter a tenant who deliberately withholds payments from us. If they are late in paying, it is mostly because of financial irresponsibility. Their ability to manage their finances is sometimes poor and this goes back to the very reason they are our lease-option tenants. Conventional lenders will not work with them.

Additionally, we are not landlords who believe in picking up tenants' rent payments at their residence. They must mail or deliver their payments. Too many smaller landlords get caught up chasing their rents. Not us, we make collection efforts, but we do not pick up their payments. If they cannot pay or are unwilling to pay, they will be penalized for it.

If they are late, we insist our tenants pay the late fees. Occasionally, we are lenient especially if they have a good payment record. But enforcing the late fees serve as a deterrent and additional motivation for them to pay us on a timely basis.

If They Must Move, Arrange to Leave on Good Terms

Sometimes our tenants have to move on because they encounter financial difficulties and cannot maintain their monthly payments to us. If this occurs, it is often disappointing because they will have lost the money and time they put into the property.

However, we tell them it is always better to work out some agreeable terms on their departure, otherwise we will be compelled to use legal measures. Many times, that is motivation enough. They do not want us to come after them legally.

Support Team

We have a support team of professionals who assists us in our management responsibilities. We take great comfort in knowing we have a team of knowledgeable advisors we can turn to for expert advice.

Not only do they advise us, they also provide essential and specialized services to free up our focus so we can do what we're best at — the buying and lease-optioning of our properties.

Our advisors include the following:

- Insurance Agent
- Collection Agency
- Real Estate Broker
- Real Estate Appraiser
- Real Estate Attorney
- County Clerks
- Other Property Owners

Insurance Agent

Our insurance agent keeps us apprised of current trends in property insurance. We look to him to ensure we have adequate coverage on each property we manage or own.

Collection Agency

Although we are knowledgeable and able to handle many of the legal issues that arise (evictions, garnishments, filing suits in small claims court, etc.), we work with a collection agency to provide backup legal support. Additionally, they are better staffed to handle extended and extreme cases of default and collections if they do arise. In addition to the daily collection activities they perform such as issuing letters, making collection calls, and tracking debtors down, our collection agency have within their means the ability and wherewithal to take more aggressive measures as needed.

Real Estate Broker

Although we are quite knowledgeable regarding many of the local neighborhoods in which we work, occasionally we run into neighborhood pockets where we have less familiarity. In these situations, we look to our real estate broker to provide additional information as to the value of a given property and the general assessment of a neighborhood since they have access to recent comparable sales and property listings of the area. Our real estate broker is also good at providing leads to other reputable professionals that support the real estate profession such as contractors, inspectors, appraisers, and repair people.

Real Estate Appraiser

The real estate appraiser is a person we turn to if we need a formalized market value established for a property. The assessment service they provide can either be a drive-by appraisal or a full appraisal with inspection. Often, appraisals are used for the purpose of qualifying for conventional mortgage financing.

Real Estate Attorney

This is a given. Our real estate attorney handles the high level issues of financing, deed conveyance, contract inspections, and acquisitions. She also performs our closings of property purchases with conventional mortgage loans. More importantly, she acts as our legal representative for our management business. In cases where people do not know us, her name association along with the fact she regularly represents our interests gives credibility to our operation.

Because I live in an area where real estate professionals are generally conservative, they are less familiar with the model and operations of our business. If there is additional clarification needed as to what and how we do things, we refer interested parties to our real estate attorney.

Court Clerks

Technically, these people are not allowed to give advice. However, we have found those clerks with whom we've become familiar and friendly with, are quite helpful. Having a friendly relationship with the county clerks has been very instrumental in cases we handle in-house. They know the legal process and the court paperwork well.

They give us insights people would not normally know unless they were regular visitors to the courthouse.

Other Property Owners

As with any line of business, we inevitably encounter others who do what we do. Our business is no different. We have friends and associates who own many investment properties in other geographical markets. Because they are in a different geographical market, we do not have competitive issues. As such, we contact one another, "talk shop" and compare notes.

We find these relationships to be very helpful in getting another investor's perspective.

It is important to note, even though our advisors help us in their respective areas, they are not investors or property managers. As such, they do not necessarily have the same perspective or priorities we do when compared to other investment property owners. Conversing with other property owners allow us to share ideas to deal with common issues.

Contract Helpers

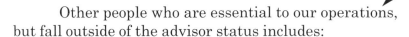

Other people who are essential to our operations, but fall outside of the advisor status includes:

- Handyman
- Housekeeper
- Landscaper
- Property Inspector

We cultivate a steady working relationship with these workers. Although they work on a contract, as-needed basis, we make sure we give our business to them time and time again. Why? We get higher priority as a preferred client with consistent pricing and quality of work.

Investment Partners

The term "investment partner" is a generic term I use for people we work with who provide financial resources to buy investment property. Early in my investment career, I quickly realized that no one person would have access to all the capital needed to buy investment properties.

As such, I quickly sought out investment partners to accelerate the growth of my portfolio. It was this limitation that encouraged me to invite Wes Weaver, my business partner, to join forces with me in property management.

In theory, there are an infinite number of ways to work with investment partners. In fact, we have done it in a variety of ways depending on the people who were interested in our lease-option management style of cash flowing properties.

Some have provided cash while we sought the financing. Others have provided both cash and their credit to qualify for the mortgage loans. In all cases, we prefer simplicity.

Today, we have transitioned to an "all-cash" model to work with investment partners, since it is the simplest way of all. We still continue to acquire property using seller-financing, and occasionally we find someone to qualify for a loan, but it is a slow and inefficient process.

We now seek out interested parties who receive low returns (less than 5%) in savings accounts and certificates of deposit but want a higher return (8%-10%) without substantially losing the safety they already have.

We have an Informational Audio CD we send to qualified investors interested in our investment programs. Visit www.turnkeyinvesting.com for more information.

People who have substantial funds in their retirement accounts or 5-year certificates of deposit are good candidates. We pay a *flat and guaranteed annual return* (regardless of our vacancy or other expense factors) where their money is secured by a first mortgage on the property.

As in any business, there are good investment partners and there are problematic ones. The good ones know what they want, understand the program, are decisive, want to move forward and collect their returns. They are generally optimistic but recognize there is some degree of risk in any investment program.

The problematic ones are high maintenance, indecisive, require a good amount of hand-holding, and "squirrelly" about real estate and investing in general. They are generally pessimistic and have a great need for control. Needless to say, we discourage those types of people from working with us. They are better suited investing elsewhere.

We have adopted a management philosophy of matching the investment to the investor. And if it is not a good fit, we won't use their money to buy property. It's quite simple.

If you are interested in becoming one of our investment partners and participating in the program we offer, please visit *www.turnkeyinvesting.com*. Additionally, there is additional information in the back of the book that may be helpful in exploring investment opportunities with us.

Administration

I will touch briefly on this section because it is an area of concern for anyone wanting to self-manage their own real estate portfolio.

This is an ever-changing process to streamline administration and make it simpler and more efficient. What follows is by no means the definitive way to manage the administrative duties every management company face, but it is our current method.

I am a huge proponent of using technology to maximize productivity and efficiency in our administration. In fact, much of our administration is dependent on technology. It is amazing to me how people got anything done years ago before we had all this technology. Back then, they had to hire a lot more people. A few people today can do so much with the right hardware and software.

High-speed Internet Access

Equally amazing is how many people still use dial-up analog lines for Internet access. For us, paying for high-speed Internet access is very inexpensive for the value we get.

Not only do we have quick access to our own marketing websites for updates, but we have the ability to quickly send photos, contracts, letters, and a variety of data to each other and our support team.

With high-speed Internet access, that connection can be expanded to accommodate multiple users with the use of an inexpensive Internet router. Besides, with more audio and video on the Internet, it is practically impossible to download large multimedia files with only a dial-up analog connection.

In addition, a dedicated, high-speed Internet connection frees up the need for an extra phone line.

Local Area Network

For offices with more than one computer, it is almost impossible to operate efficiently without installing a small local area network to share files and information. Today, networking hardware is quite inexpensive, and it is often built into many computers. All that is needed is an additional router and some cables to connect the computers together. I still prefer cabled networking for non-mobile, in-house computers.

We currently use Microsoft Windows XP, which includes the networking software. Microsoft networking is easy to configure and install once all the hardware and connections are in place.

Property Management Software

Because we manage a fairly sizable portfolio of investment property, we utilize property management software that specializes in software management of rental property, leases, tenants, utilities, reporting, and so forth.

Conventional accounting software is simply too clumsy and inefficient to do what we need it to do. The property management software I recommend is PropertyBoss which is available for sale on our website.

General Accounting Software

Although property management software is quite good at managing the property aspects, it is not good for general business accounting and bookkeeping where financial statements and reporting are needed.

There are many reputable accounting software programs available today. For smaller businesses, I recommend Peachtree Accounting, MYOB Accounting, and QuickBooks. They are well-supported and established in the marketplace. My personal preference, however, is QuickBooks.

When you choose your accounting software, keep in mind what your bookkeeper and tax specialist prefer to use. After all, unless you are an accountant and plan to do your own taxes, you will have to coordinate your data and reports with your accounting team members.

Filing System

Because management of a real estate portfolio is still paper intensive, a well thought out filing system is essential. This is the only major part of our administration that is almost entirely hand-based. There are some things that technology cannot replace. Documents, contracts, statements, receipts, and other paperwork must be tracked, organized, and filed.

Our property management filing system consists of the following:

Acquisitions Files
These files contain paperwork relating to the acquisition of the investment property. This file is not accessed frequently after the purchase of a property is completed. Much of the paperwork here is for reference and archival purposes.

Tenant Files
These files contain our lease-option paperwork as well as copies of late notices, record of payments, and evictions. These tenant files are separate from the other property-related files because this file sees the most activity on a monthly basis.

Administrative Files
These files contain property tax notices, utilities, expenses, mortgage statements, and insurance paperwork. These files are occasionally accessed but not frequent enough to combine with our Tenant files.

Summary

The area of administration is so broad and diverse; it can vary greatly from one office to another even in the same line of business. We have included ongoing Tenant Management as part of the administration process.

What we have outlined is only a baseline to work from. The specifics of implementation will largely be dependent on the work done within a team. The way we do administration continues to improve and evolve. It is something we pay close attention to as we continue to grow our property portfolio. We aim for simplicity and efficiency every step of the way.

Written Exercise – Part 1

Did I truly understand the main points of this chapter? What do I need to review again?

Which ideas in this chapter can I adapt to my market?

Which ideas in this chapter can I start implementing immediately?

Written Exercise – Part 2

Which tasks do I need to do myself? Which tasks do I need to delegate to others?

What team members do I need to contact to assist me in implementing the ideas within this chapter?

What follow-up questions do I need to ask the Author? What additional information do I need to research?

11 The TurnKey Investing Philosophy

This book was written to provide inside information on how we utilize and implement the lease-options strategy to manage our investment portfolio in our base area of Columbus, Georgia / Phenix City, Alabama. All the "how to" information we provided herein is driven by the management philosophy we adopted and follow. In fact, we refer to it as *"The TurnKey Investing Philosophy"*.

Our Strategy

With the exception of my first half-dozen properties, the growth of our portfolio has been accomplished as a joint effort between my business partner, Wes Weaver and myself. We accomplish much more as a team than separately. We do deals together and manage properties together. We believe in utilizing the concept of "divide-and-conquer" if and when it is appropriate and serves us. However, we also firmly adhere to the concept of "strength in numbers" especially when certain situations arise and must be handled.

We've only made small efforts to give insight on how to adapt what we have done into another real estate marketplace. Why? There is simply too much diversity in different real estate markets throughout the United States for any one book or author to cover adequately.

Therefore, I chose to write about our expertise; the bread-and-butter we actively pursue each and every day and how we do it. Nothing more, nothing less. We consider ourselves experts at what we do where we are and nowhere else. Despite this, I believe astute readers will pick up points and information from this book to apply to their own situation.

Staying Focused

It has been our choice to succeed in our vision with laser-beam focus in the Columbus, Georgia / Phenix City, Alabama area because we wanted to become #1 with Owner-financed houses through lease-options.

Does this mean if Wes and I were suddenly transplanted to another city, we couldn't learn, master, and become experts there? Of course not. In fact, we feel we can adapt to just about any real estate market if we had to. We believe our experience and achievements can be applied to many real estate markets.

The TurnKey Investing Philosophy

The reason I bring all this up is to illustrate the major points of what we believe TurnKey Investing is all about.

- Do What You are Good at Doing
- Know Your Market Well

- Invest as a Team, Never Invest Alone
- Management Drives the Success of Every Investment
- Match the Investor to the Investment
- Use a System that Works
- Perfect the System with Kaizen
- Make it Easy for Investors to Invest
- Manage Investor Money More Carefully Than Our Own Money
- Invest in the Management as much as in the Property
- Better to Make No Investment Than a Bad Investment
- Always Tell the Bad With the Good
- Be Firm but Fair

Do What You are Good at Doing

One of the dangers we've seen is straying too far away from what you're good at doing. It doesn't mean we cannot be good at more than one thing. Instead, it means we have developed an awareness of the things we can do with great confidence and certainty of success, compared to those things we do with less certainty and greater risk.

There are people in this world who are very good at making money in their businesses but not very good at managing or investing the money they make. These people should recognize this fact and seek out people who are good at managing and investing their money for them.

What we are good at doing is managing and cash flowing investment properties with lease-options in Columbus, Georgia and Phenix City, Alabama. At the risk of sounding boastful, we would be selling ourselves short if we did not acknowledge our success.

Know Your Market Well

We pride ourselves on the fact that we know our real estate market well. We live in a smaller city so it makes it possible for us to learn and master the marketplace compared to a large city where only a section of the market can be learned and mastered.

In the context of real estate investments, we believe some forms of investing (such as lease-options) are more conducive to certain markets than others. For example, we believe implementing lease-options as an investment strategy favors small to mid-size U.S. cities but not large or highly-appreciating cities. ***Sometimes it is better to invest money outside of where you live, not where you are.*** In my case, I chose to move to a place that was suitable for my investment strategy.

Invest with a Team, Never Invest Alone

Every investment inherently has some level of risk associated with it. There is no such thing as a risk-free investment just like there is no such thing as risk-free driving. If you get on the road to drive, there is always a small chance you will get into an accident. If you invest, there is always a small chance something will go wrong no matter how many precautions you take.

However, it is important to note risks can be mitigated when more than one person bears the responsibility of an investment. Wes and I have chosen to invest our money together; we have also chosen to manage our properties together. This way, there is always a fallback position.

As we have previously mentioned, it is key to have a team of professionals such as a real estate attorney, local contacts, banker, real estate agent, and others in supporting roles.

Management Drives the Success of Every Investment

One of the reasons this book has intentionally been directed to a more affluent and sophisticated investor is because they intuitively know that good managers, not the capital itself, is what drives the success of any business and investment. Poor-minded investors tend to think having money automatically determines the success of investing. If this were true, we would not hear so many stories of rock stars, sports stars, and lottery winners going broke even after coming into millions of dollars.

Having worked in NASCAR circles over ten years ago, I learned no matter how well a race car is built, how good the engine is, or how fast the car can go, the race is only won with the right driver. It doesn't mean the car is unimportant, but without a great driver, no races are ever won.

Likewise, in investing, having access to capital is essential, but without good managers watching and driving the capital and investments, both are doomed to fail.

Match the Investor to the Investment

Because we focus on our expertise within our market, we are cognizant of what we can do with a potential investor and what we cannot. We also know different people have different priorities and personal dispositions.

While we want to be exposed to many good candidates that may be interested in investing with us, we also know only a select few people will actually be suitable. We have a very specific niche we fulfill, and only certain investors are suitable for this type of investment.

For example, we now seek "cash-only" investment partners. We rarely seek investors who want to qualify for mortgage loans. Although we will occasionally work with some individuals who prefer to qualify for a loan, it is not our primary focus.

Just like how we choose suitable clothes to fit our style, we look for investors who are suitable for our investments. We match the investor to the investments we have.

Use a System That Works

We allocate time to look for ways to improve and streamline our existing system, as well as continue to refine our implementation procedures. At the same time, we are selling lease-options to our tenants. Having said that, once we have developed a good working system for our market, we use it over and over again.

The best example is how we market our properties through *ownerfinancehomes.com* where we advertise the property, our website, our firm, and our niche simultaneously. It is a very good, cost-effective marketing system that gets better with maturity.

It has worked well, continues to work well, and we continue to expand on it.

Perfect the System with Kaizen

We are firm believers in practicing the Japanese concept of Kaizen. The concept of Kaizen is the belief of making small, ongoing improvements to a business system, which over time, nets great results.

Practicing Kaizen is not always about being the fastest sprinter or making large changes to a system. It is about finishing the marathon as a winner. Sometimes finishing the marathon successfully is not about speed. It is about steadily making progress throughout the entire race.

We are constantly refining how we manage our investment properties, our tenants, and the support team we work with.

Make it Easy for Investors to Invest

This is something we are passionate about. We believe investors want to simply and safely invest their money and receive good steady returns on their money. We also believe the investing experience must be a positive one.

Unfortunately, the general nature of real estate makes it somewhat more involved than stock investments. However, this does not mean it has to be a painful experience.

We have two programs we provide to those who want to invest funds with us. One is an "all-cash" Private Lender Program; the other is a "cash plus credit program" Loan Qualification Program, which we only do on a case-by-case basis.

By far, we prefer to work with people on the "all-cash" Private Lender program since it bypasses the tedious mortgage loan qualifying process. While we do everything we can to make the loan qualifying process painless, there are many aspects of the process we cannot control.

With the Private Lender program, we are able to control most of the process. So, investing with us is a more positive and pleasant experience.

Manage Investor Money More Carefully Than Our Own Money

We feel a greater weight of fiduciary responsibility to invest more carefully when using investor funds. Our business is highly dependent on "repeat investors" and "word of mouth" referrals. And we encourage this. As such, we have a vested interest in closely guarding our reputations.

For example, if we used an investment partner's financial resources to take on borderline investment properties and they did not perform well, we create the potential for long-term damage to our reputations. While personal reputation is relatively unimportant to some, we greatly value ours. No deal is worth damaging our reputations over.

It is quite common for us to either decline borderline investment opportunities or use our own financial resources to "test" or "guinea pig" properties we are interested in before placing investor funds into it. Any financial setbacks that could occur would impact no one but us. As such, we take a more conservative approach when using investor funds than our own funds.

Invest in the Management as Much as in the Property

There are two ways of looking at this. We have always known how well we perform as property managers determines how well our investments perform. After all, management drives the success of the investment.

As such, we have committed financial resources to set up more effective management systems. These include management and accounting software. In addition, we also work with vendors who provide services to support our ability to manage. We actively cultivate relationships through familiarity with staff members in the court system and the banks we deal with.

As an investor, you will have many investment opportunities presented to you. However, you should ask yourself the following questions:

- How much access will I have to the principals of the management team?
- Do the principals value their reputation?
- Are they selective with whom they work with or will they work with anyone who has money?
- Do they value working relationships or do they only value my money?
- Will they go beyond the call of duty?
- How much do the principals have vested with the company and their portfolio of properties?
- Do they have references and other credibility materials?
- Do they have a strong support network?

Getting answers to these questions will help you make a good decision as to whom you should work with and not solely base the decision on a rate of return. After all, there will be many investment opportunities you will be exposed to which will have similar rates of return. The deciding factor will be the Management Team you choose to work and spend your time with.

Better to Make No Investment than a Bad Investment

In the aftermath of the Technology Stocks Crash of 2000, there are many who have been humbled. In 1999, if you offered to pay someone 5% return on their investment, they probably would have been laughed out the door. Today, if you ask someone who lost money in the years after 2000 if they could go back and earn 5% instead of speculating on stocks, they would jump at the chance. In fact, those who lost tremendously would be more than happy to have broken even with a 0% return. Hindsight is almost always 20/20.

However, this is truly a sad sight to see. The whole point of investing is to create returns, not hoping to break even. But that is what many people today are saying. They wished they had broken even so they didn't have to take the loss.

The reality is they dealt with investment managers who had no control over the market or the investments they were promoting. If those investors had not been overly speculative, they probably would not have lost their money. The fact is, speculative stocks are often bad investments. You either win big or lose big. It sounds like gambling to me.

Fortunately, because of the niche we are in, we do have influence over the marketplace. Even so, we do not offer huge speculative rates of returns. We offer good investments with steady rates of return. It gives us something clear and predictable to work with. More importantly, the investor gets a steady return they can count on month in and month out. Personally, I think every investment portfolio should have such elements of safety and stability.

Always Tell the Bad with the Good

I have always disliked people who sell a fairy tale story where everything always turns out good. They never tell the downside of a story.

In investing, there is always a risk, the downside. The extreme downside is obvious. You could lose all your money! Experienced investors know that investing involves some degree of risk. However, the question is what is being done to mitigate the risk.

Telling the bad side is not about being pessimistic or cynical. Telling the bad side in the context of investing is being upfront with all parties as to the potential risks and downsides of a particular investment. It makes good business sense.

We're upfront and tell both sides of the story. But it still goes without saying we are clearly confident and optimistic in what we do. (Otherwise, why would we continue to stay in this business?)

Be Firm but Fair

As investment managers and investors ourselves, we have a clear bias towards the investor. Investment partners help fuel the growth of our acquisitions. However, it is our tenants who make an investment perform. So we take this into consideration.

As property managers, we walk a fine line between taking care of the investor and being fair to our tenants. After all, there are rules and laws to abide by with our tenants. Even if this were not the case, our tenants are the people who make the payment, which allow our investments to perform.

We are not absolutely ruthless, nor are we unforgiving of our tenants. Why? Many times it is simply not in our best interest to do so.

We exercise a firm but fair management philosophy not only with our tenants, but the vendors we work with.

Summary

Within every successful investment portfolio, there is a winning philosophy that guides the actions of the management team. We are no different. As the title of the book indicates, we advocate a "turnkey" approach to doing things. More specifically, we have developed a turnkey system of doing lease-options; it works for our investment partners and us.

Our portfolio continues to perform well month in and month out. And while there are occasional setbacks both in management and performance, we are happy to report success in our ventures.

Our *Turnkey Investing Philosophy* allows for both change and growth, and it helps keep us grounded. We believe every successful management team should put into writing a management philosophy that they can share with others. It helps the management team to be accountable to themselves and the people they work with. In the end, it is all about setting the right expectations for all involved and then delivering solid results.

Written Exercise – Part 1

Did I truly understand the main points of this chapter? What do I need to review again?

Which ideas in this chapter can I adapt to my market?

Which ideas in this chapter can I start implementing immediately?

Written Exercise – Part 2

Which tasks do I need to do myself? Which tasks do I need to delegate to others?

What team members do I need to contact to assist me in implementing the ideas within this chapter?

What follow-up questions do I need to ask the Author? What additional information do I need to research?

In Conclusion

As with all endeavors, there must be a stopping point. Writing a book is no different. I resisted the temptation to go back and "add just one more thing". And so, we have come to the end of this book.

I tend to believe in life there are always things that could have been done better. In the case of this book, was this the best book I could have written on how we implement the lease-option strategy to create a profitable investment portfolio? I can easily answer that. The answer is "No".

I say this for two reasons. One, I had to stop somewhere otherwise the book would never be completed. Two, I am not a professional writer despite the fact that I am an author. I am foremost an entrepreneur and investor who occasionally writes a book.

Like I said in the Introduction, I believe there is a platinum-mine of great information here and the information herein is easily worth 100 times the cover price of this book.

Although the subject matter is primarily centered on the lease-option strategy, the primary objective stated on the book cover is *"How to Simply and Safely Create 12% Returns with Investment Property!"* From this view, I believe I have not only shown but also proven that it can be done easily.

There is a saying I have heard; people should "eat their own dog food". What that saying means is that any company should be able to confidently use whatever product or service they provide for their customers.

Having read my own chapters many times during the writing and editing process, I made sure that the information herein was consistent and accurate to what we do. Questions I asked myself were:

- Can I confidently give this book to someone new within our organization to jumpstart their training?
- Can I proudly give this book to new investment partners and let them know, in a way few people can, what and how we do things?

I can confidently, proudly, and unquestionably declare, "Yes, I can".

Writing this book has been one of my greatest challenges in recent years. Trying to take a complicated and tedious subject with many moving and ever-changing elements and then distilling it into a 200-page book is not easy. Whether I have done a good job by you, the reader, only you can say.

What I would like to point out is that there is a difference between talking about what we do vs. what others do. We believe there is no one else better qualified to tell others what we do better than we can. And if we are not willing to do it, then it won't happen. Wes and I live this on a daily basis and we believe the time was right for this book to be published.

As in my previous book, I invite you to freely provide feedback to me. I hope you took the time to write down questions you want answered and points you want clarified. Maybe you are even interested in becoming one of our investment partners. Regardless, I want to hear from you.

Writing a book can sometimes be a lonely endeavor. But one of the benefits I hope to reap is being able to interact and get feedback from you, the reader. Thank you for reading this book.

Until we meet next time, may all your investments be simple, safe, and steady.

Matthew S. Chan

Appendix A: Sample Documents

I have provided three sample documents from our Contracts & Forms package for educational purposes. These documents were specially created in response to our local tenant market and situations that arose in the field. The actual appearance and formatting vary somewhat from the actual document.

- Property Inspection Affidavit
- Administrative Fee Agreement
- Lease Addendum for Appliances

We periodically update and add new forms to our contracts and agreements package. If you are interested in purchasing our Contracts and Forms package which comes with a full year of free updates, visit ***www.turnkeyinvesting.com*** for more information.

PROPERTY INSPECTION AFFIDAVIT

Property: 123 ABC Street, Anywhere USA

We understand the property is being leased with an option-to-buy in an "as is" condition.

In this transaction, we understand the Landlord has made reasonable efforts to disclose any general defects in the areas of appearance, systems functionality, and structural integrity of the Property.

We understand that while reasonable efforts have been made by the Landlord to provide accurate information regarding the condition, functionality, and structural integrity of the Property, it is OUR responsibility to make the necessary arrangements for professional inspection to OUR satisfaction.

We understand that the purpose of a property inspection is NOT for the intent to compel the Landlord to make corrections or improvements of any discovered defects or deficiencies. It is for the purpose of deciding whether or not I will consummate the transaction and accept the responsibilities at the agreed upon terms of the lease and option.

We understand that if we do not arrange for professional property inspection, we do so of our own free will and fully accept the responsibilities of any undiscovered defects and deficiencies.

We fully acknowledge that the Landlord has given us sufficient time and access to fully inspect the Property as to its overall condition including but not limited to: overall appearance, systems functionality, and structural integrity.

By signing this affidavit, we acknowledge that we (or our hired professional inspectors) have fully inspected the property to our satisfaction. We hereby fully accept the property and the responsibilities thereof in "as is" condition and there will be NO REFUNDS of any monies paid in.

______________________________ __________________

Tenant Date

Disclaimer: *This sample document has been provided for educational purposes. We assume no liability whatsoever for any direct or indirect consequences for use of this sample document.*

ADMINISTRATIVE FEE AGREEMENT

Property: 123 ABC Street, Anywhere USA

We fully acknowledge that the Landlord is providing a valuable service of providing a Lease with Option-to-Buy transaction.

As a consequence, I fully understand and agree that the Landlord has charged a **non-refundable** $200.00 administrative fee that is NOT applicable towards any rent, option money, or security deposit.

________________________________ ____________________

Tenant Date

Disclaimer: *This sample document has been provided for educational purposes. We assume no liability whatsoever for any direct or indirect consequences for use of this sample document.*

LEASE ADDENDUM FOR APPLIANCES

Property: 123 ABC Street, Anywhere, USA

I hereby acknowledge that the following appliances have been provided to me for rental use:

_______ Air-conditioning Window Units

_______ Stove

_______ Refrigerator

_______ Dishwasher

I agree to use and maintain these appliances with reasonable care.

In the event of voluntary or involuntary move out and appliances are missing, I understand that the Landlord will assume the Tenant has committed a criminal act of theft that will be promptly reported to the local Sheriff's Office and the City Police Department and that prosecution fully allowed by the law will be pursued.

As a remedy for any missing appliances, the Tenant may provide a new replacement unit ONLY if the Landlord approves the replacement. No used replacements will be honored without special permission and consideration.

This notice has been read to me and I fully understand the statements herein.

______________________________ ________________

Tenant Date

Disclaimer: *This sample document has been provided for educational purposes. We assume no liability whatsoever for any direct or indirect consequences for use of this sample document.*

Appendix B: Area Maps

Regional Map

Columbus, Georgia and Phenix City , Alabama Area

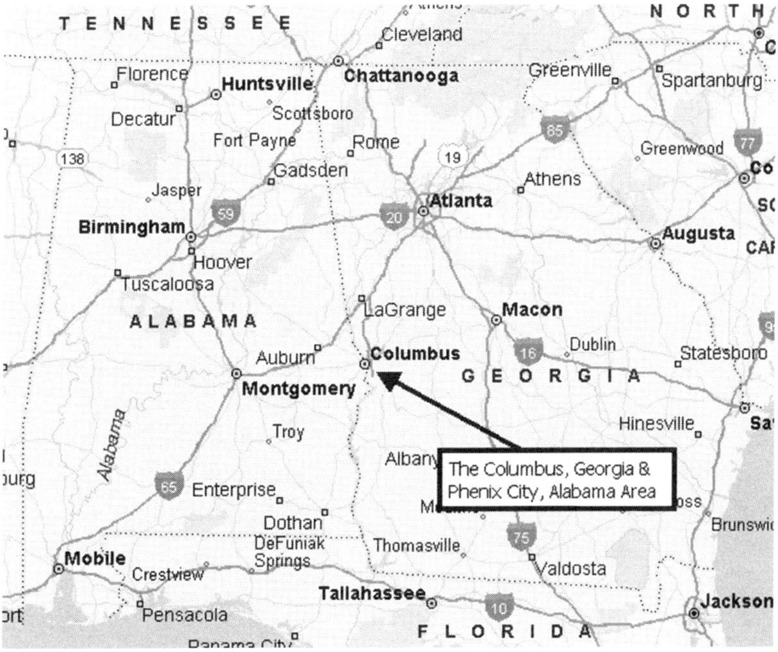

The Greater Columbus Area
(Columbus, Georgia & Phenix City, Alabama)

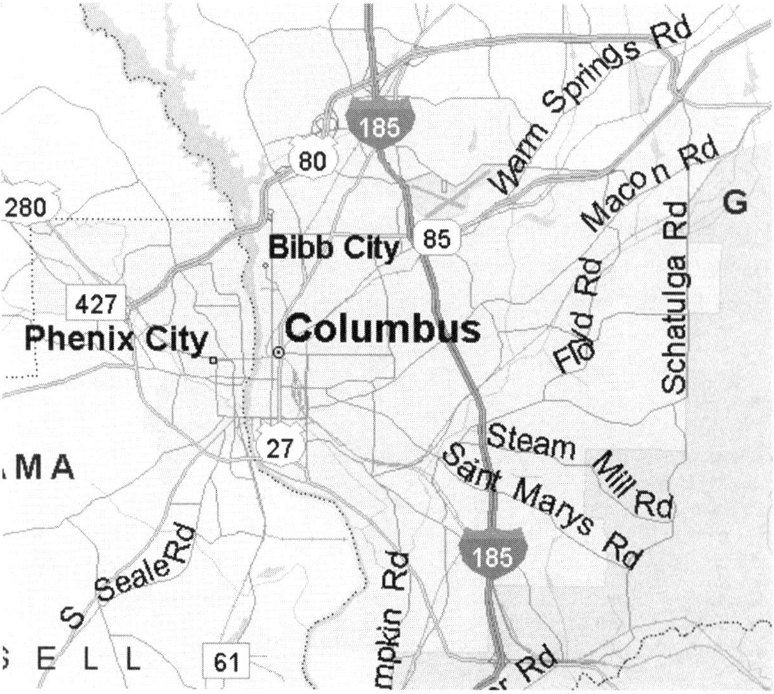

Appendix C: Area Demographics

I have provided demographic information of the Greater Columbus, Georgia area; the local market we invest in. The Greater Columbus, Georgia area as I have defined it here consists of the cities of Columbus, Georgia and Phenix City, Alabama.

The purpose of providing demographic information here is two-fold.

- It provides a guideline to information you may want to research and analyze as described in Chapter 3.
- The information provides a snapshot and overview of our local market for those of you who may be interested in becoming investment partners with us.

The information provided herein originally came from the Year 2000 U.S. Census (*www.census.gov*). The information was compiled from two sets of data, one for Columbus, Georgia, and the other for Phenix City, Alabama. Each set of data from the two cities were then combined to form one "Combined Area" which I denote as the Greater Columbus, Georgia area.

	Columbus, GA		Phenix City, AL		Combined Area	
TOTAL POPULATION	**185,781**	**100.0%**	**28,265**	**100.0%**	**214,046**	**100.0%**
Gender						
Male	90,375	48.6%	13,082	46.3%	103,457	48.3%
Female	95,406	51.4%	15,183	53.7%	110,589	51.7%
Median age (years)	*32.6*	*X*	*35.1*	*X*		*X*
18 years and over	135,902	73.2%	20,837	73.7%	156,739	73.2%
Male	64,990	35.0%	9,289	32.9%	74,279	34.7%
Female	70,912	38.2%	11,548	40.9%	82,460	38.5%

	Columbus, GA		Phenix City, AL		Combined Area	
HOUSEHOLD INCOME (1999)						
Total Households	**69,787**	**100.0%**	**11,525**	**100.0%**	**81,312**	**100.0%**
Less than $10,000	8,564	12.3%	2,373	20.6%	10,937	13.5%
$10,000 to $14,999	5,314	7.6%	1,138	9.9%	6,452	7.9%
$15,000 to $24,999	10,791	15.5%	1,856	16.1%	12,647	15.6%
$25,000 to $34,999	10,387	14.9%	1,596	13.8%	11,983	14.7%
$35,000 to $49,999	11,875	17.0%	1,900	16.5%	13,775	16.9%
$50,000 to $74,999	12,209	17.5%	1,593	13.8%	13,802	17.0%
$75,000 to $99,999	5,081	7.3%	682	5.9%	5,763	7.1%
$100,000 to $149,999	3,698	5.3%	256	2.2%	3,954	4.9%
$150,000 to $199,999	710	1.0%	77	0.7%	787	1.0%
$200,000 or more	1,158	1.7%	54	0.5%	1,212	1.5%
Median household income (dollars)	*34,798*	*X*	*26,720*	*X*		*X*

	Columbus, GA		Phenix City, AL		Combined Area	
HOUSEHOLDS BY TYPE						
Total households	**69,599**	**100.0%**	**11,517**	**100.0%**	**81,116**	**100.0%**
Family households (families)	47,560	68.3%	7,569	65.7%	55,129	68.0%
With own children under 18 years	24,102	34.6%	3,646	31.7%	27,748	34.2%
Married-couple family	31,106	44.7%	4,538	39.4%	35,644	43.9%
With own children under 18 years	14,412	20.7%	1,878	16.3%	16,290	20.1%
Female householder, no husband present	13,628	19.6%	2,545	22.1%	16,173	19.9%
With own children under 18 years	8,253	11.9%	1,550	13.5%	9,803	12.1%
Nonfamily households	22,039	31.7%	3,948	34.3%	25,987	32.0%
Householder living alone	18,579	26.7%	3,497	30.4%	22,076	27.2%
Householder 65 years and over	6,517	9.4%	1,319	11.5%	7,836	9.7%
Households with individuals under 18 years	27,259	39.2%	4,157	36.1%	31,416	38.7%
Households with individuals 65 years and over	15,791	22.7%	2,955	25.7%	18,746	23.1%

Appendix C ➢ *Area Demographics*

	Columbus, GA		*Phenix City, AL*		*Combined Area*	
Employed civilian population 16 years and over	**75,476**	**100.0%**	**11,323**	**100.0%**	**86,799**	**100.0%**
OCCUPATION						
Management, professional, and related occupations	23,160	30.7%	3,181	28.1%	26,341	30.3%
Service occupations	12,663	16.8%	1,631	14.4%	14,294	16.5%
Sales and office occupations	20,149	26.7%	3,039	26.8%	23,188	26.7%
Farming, fishing, and forestry occupations	136	0.2%	35	0.3%	171	0.2%
Construction, extraction, and maintenance occupations	6,884	9.1%	1,086	9.6%	7,970	9.2%
Production, transportation, and material moving occupations	12,484	16.5%	2,351	20.8%	14,835	17.1%
INDUSTRY						
Agriculture, forestry, fishing and hunting, and mining	322	0.4%	62	0.5%	384	0.4%
Construction	4,524	6.0%	761	6.7%	5,285	6.1%
Manufacturing	11,218	14.9%	2,272	20.1%	13,490	15.5%
Wholesale trade	1,533	2.0%	290	2.6%	1,823	2.1%
Retail trade	8,726	11.6%	1,330	11.7%	10,056	11.6%
Transportation and warehousing, and utilities	2,733	3.6%	389	3.4%	3,122	3.6%
Information	2,084	2.8%	265	2.3%	2,349	2.7%
Finance, insurance, real estate, and rental and leasing	8,150	10.8%	1,142	10.1%	9,292	10.7%
Professional, scientific, management, administrative, and waste management services	4,560	6.0%	710	6.3%	5,270	6.1%
Educational, health and social services	16,205	21.5%	2,135	18.9%	18,340	21.1%
Arts, entertainment, recreation, accommodation and food services	6,821	9.0%	748	6.6%	7,569	8.7%
Other services (except public administration)	4,064	5.4%	504	4.5%	4,568	5.3%
Public administration	4,536	6.0%	715	6.3%	5,251	6.0%
CLASS OF WORKER						
Private wage and salary workers	56,871	75.3%	8,892	78.5%	65,763	75.8%
Government workers	14,402	19.1%	1,903	16.8%	16,305	18.8%
Self-employed workers in own not incorporated business	3,992	5.3%	472	4.2%	4,464	5.1%
Unpaid family workers	211	0.3%	56	0.5%	267	0.3%

	Columbus, GA		Phenix City, AL		Combined Area	
HOUSING OCCUPANCY						
Total housing units	**75,940**	**100.0%**	**13,250**	**100.0%**	**89,190**	**100.0%**
Occupied housing units	69,599	91.6%	11,517	86.9%	81,116	90.9%
Vacant housing units	6,341	8.4%	1,733	13.1%	8,074	9.1%
For seasonal, recreational, or occasional use	206	0.3%	25	0.2%	231	0.3%
(percent)	*2*	*X*	*4*	*X*		*X*
Rental vacancy rate (percent)	*11*	*X*	*16*	*X*		*X*
HOUSING TENURE						
Occupied housing units	**69,599**	**100.0%**	**11,517**	**100.0%**	**81,116**	**100.0%**
Owner-occupied housing units	39,244	56.4%	6,067	52.7%	45,311	55.9%
Renter-occupied housing units	30,355	43.6%	5,450	47.3%	35,805	44.1%

	Columbus, GA		Phenix City, AL		Combined Area	
TENURE BY BEDROOMS						
Owner-occupied housing units	**39,266**	**100.0%**	**6,005**	**100.0%**	**45,271**	**100.0%**
No bedroom	193	0.5%	14	0.2%	207	0.5%
1 bedroom	836	2.1%	183	3.0%	1,019	2.3%
2 bedrooms	5,898	15.0%	1,396	23.2%	7,294	16.1%
3 bedrooms	24,042	61.2%	3,534	58.9%	27,576	60.9%
4 bedrooms	7,299	18.6%	766	12.8%	8,065	17.8%
5 or more bedrooms	998	2.5%	112	1.9%	1,110	2.5%
Renter-occupied housing units	**30,331**	**100.0%**	**5,519**	**100.0%**	**35,850**	**100.0%**
No bedroom	1,057	3.5%	78	1.4%	1,135	3.2%
1 bedroom	7,040	23.2%	1,461	26.5%	8,501	23.7%
2 bedrooms	12,953	42.7%	2,703	49.0%	15,656	43.7%
3 bedrooms	8,312	27.4%	1,114	20.2%	9,426	26.3%
4 bedrooms	836	2.8%	156	2.8%	992	2.8%
5 or more bedrooms	133	0.4%	7	0.1%	140	0.4%

	Columbus, GA		Phenix City, AL		Combined Area	
Specified renter-occupied units	**30,220**	**100.0%**	**5,519**	**100.0%**	**35,739**	**100.0%**
GROSS RENT						
Less than $200	2,158	7.1%	842	15.3%	3,000	8.4%
$200 to $299	2,379	7.9%	694	12.6%	3,073	8.6%
$300 to $499	9,367	31.0%	1,830	33.2%	11,197	31.3%
$500 to $749	10,633	35.2%	1,590	28.8%	12,223	34.2%
$750 to $999	2,555	8.5%	238	4.3%	2,793	7.8%
$1,000 to $1,499	586	1.9%	51	0.9%	637	1.8%
$1,500 or more	157	0.5%	-	0.0%	157	0.4%
No cash rent	2,385	7.9%	274	5.0%	2,659	7.4%
Median (dollars)	*500*	*X*	*431*	*X*	*931*	*X*

	Columbus, GA		Phenix City, AL		Combined Area	
Specified owner-occupied units	**36,314**	**100.0%**	**5,664**	**100.0%**	**41,978**	**100.0%**
VALUE						
Less than $50,000	4,867	13.4%	1,253	22.1%	6,120	14.6%
$50,000 to $99,999	18,958	52.2%	3,074	54.3%	22,032	52.5%
$100,000 to $149,999	7,149	19.7%	847	15.0%	7,996	19.0%
$150,000 to $199,999	2,693	7.4%	291	5.1%	2,984	7.1%
$200,000 to $299,999	1,829	5.0%	162	2.9%	1,991	4.7%
$300,000 to $499,999	555	1.5%	8	0.1%	563	1.3%
$500,000 to $999,999	215	0.6%	6	0.1%	221	0.5%
$1,000,000 or more	48	0.1%	23	0.4%	71	0.2%
Median (dollars)	*84,100*	*X*	*73,000*	*X*	*157,100*	*X*

	Columbus, GA		Phenix City, AL		Combined Area	
MORTGAGE STATUS						
All Houses, Any Status	**36,314**	**100.0%**	**5,664**	**100.0%**	**41,978**	**100.0%**
With a mortgage, contract to purchase, or similar debt	26,511	73.0%	3,514	62.0%	30,025	71.5%
With a second mortgage or home equity loan, but not both	6,416	24.2%	545	15.5%	6,961	23.2%
Second mortgage only	3,939	14.9%	335	9.5%	4,274	14.2%
Home equity loan only	2,477	9.3%	210	6.0%	2,687	8.9%
Both second mortgage and home equity loan	91	0.3%	18	0.5%	109	0.4%
No second mortgage or home equity loan	20,004	75.5%	2,951	84.0%	22,955	76.5%
Without a mortgage	9,803	27.0%	2,150	38.0%	11,953	28.5%

	Columbus, GA		Phenix City, AL		Combined Area	
MONTHLY MORTGAGE OWNER COSTS						
All Houses, Any Status	**36,314**	**100.0%**	**5,664**	**100.0%**	**41,978**	**100.0%**
With a mortgage	26,511	73.0%	3,514	62.0%	30,025	71.5%
Less than $300	410	1.1%	84	1.5%	494	1.2%
$300 to $499	2,350	6.5%	652	11.5%	3,002	7.2%
$500 to $699	5,325	14.7%	883	15.6%	6,208	14.8%
$700 to $999	8,486	23.4%	1,124	19.8%	9,610	22.9%
$1,000 to $1,499	6,892	19.0%	532	9.4%	7,424	17.7%
$1,500 to $1,999	1,912	5.3%	170	3.0%	2,082	5.0%
$2,000 or more	1,136	3.1%	69	1.2%	1,205	2.9%
Median (dollars)	*872*	*X*	*729*	*X*	*1,601*	*X*
Not mortgaged	9,803	27.0%	2,150	38.0%	11,953	28.5%
Median (dollars)	*231*	*X*	*208*	*X*	*439*	*X*

Acknowledgements

I most want to recognize my friend, business partner, and lead contributor of this book, Wes Weaver. Wes is the man who most responsible for helping me create and implement the "turnkey" into "TurnKey Investing". Without his help, I could not have accomplished what I have done today. Nor could I have written this book.

With Wes at my side, I am proud to say we have made a formidable team in the Greater Columbus, Georgia area. This book is a testament to his huge contributions to our business and investments. I thank Wes for coming into my life those years ago to support me both personally and professionally today.

There are other people I would like to acknowledge:

To those teachers who have most influenced and impacted me with their business acumen, technical knowledge, and investment wisdom. Their combined teachings helped shape the investment style I have today. I thank John Burley, Bill Bronchick, Van Tharp, and Keith Cunningham.

To my investor friends who continue to support my investment ventures with their advice and encouragement. Their friendship continues to inspire and propel me forward by leaps and bounds in ways they do not even realize. I thank Joe Arlt, Troy Arment, Wayne & Ros Bourke, Craig Chandler, Steve Copper, Steve Dover, Dean Edelson, Fred & Marleen Geyen, Bill Gordon, Gregg & Felicity Heffernan, Jerry & Lisa Hoganson, Damion Lupo, Brad Simmons, and Chad Watson.

To those special friends who support me and my business in their own unique way. I thank Cindy Chapin, Melita Hunt, Stephanie Olsen, Rita Canizzaro, and P.J. Zwart.

To the friends who are continually interested in what I do in my business life no matter what I do. They provide ongoing optimism for any work I do. I thank Ryan Stewart, Beverly Weaver, Paolo Bruno, Stephanie Frank, and Jack Williams.

The Creative Team

The author often receives the sole recognition and credit for the finished book. People think the author did all the work. Nothing can be further from the truth. I would like to recognize those individuals who helped me make this book possible.

First, I want to recognize my cover designer, Cheryl Edwards, for creating and transforming the cover of "TurnKey Investing with Lease-Options" into such a stunning, eye-catching piece of artwork. Her sense of creativity and flair was magical to watch as she took my descriptions and gave them visual life. More importantly, her humor for my scattered creative process is unmatched. Cheryl, I thank you and I appreciate you for the incredible patience you have shown during this past year.

Second, I want to recognize my editor, Colleen Wilson, for agreeing to take on this challenging project. She took the time to speak and advise me while keeping me updated during the whole editing process. She contributed many ideas for this book project. Colleen, I thank you and I appreciate you for how quickly you completed this project and all the feedback you gave me.

And finally, I want to give special recognition to my typesetter and desktop publisher, Deanna Reynolds, for coming to my rescue on this project. Her focus, dedication, and optimistic spirit was a joy to work with. Deanna, I thank you and I appreciate how you completed this project under less than ideal circumstances. Your contributions to this book were priceless.

To the members of the creative team, I salute them for helping me produce this book.

I recommend each of these talented individuals. You can contact them at:

Cheryl Edwards
Cover Designer / Graphic Artist
http://www.ouidzine.com

Colleen Wilson
Editor
smileywilsons@aol.com

Deanna Reynolds
Desktop Publisher/Typesetter
deannareynolds@verizon.net

About the Author

Matthew Chan is the author of "TurnKey Investing with Lease-Options", a portfolio management book that teaches independent-minded investors how to *generate safe and steady returns* through real estate and the Turnkey Lease-Option Strategy.

Matthew has been involved with investment real estate through family rental property since he was a teenager! After spending ten years in Corporate America, Matthew escaped to become a successful entrepreneur at the age of 29. A few short years later, he started his own investment real estate portfolio. Today, that highly profitable and expanding portfolio consistently generates spendable cash flow for himself and his investment partners.

Along with launching new book projects and speaking with new investment partners, Matthew continues to oversee the management of his Internet businesses and his real estate management company.

Matthew continues to enjoy the freedom of spending time working only on projects and investments with people he likes. His business and investment interests continue to take him across the U.S. where he frequently meets and networks with new people.

Matthew is also the author of "The Intrepid Way" book series. That book series teaches employees how to leave the confines of the corporate world through entrepreneurship.

Matthew's educational background includes a Bachelor of Science in Business Administration from University of Central Florida, and a Masters of Business Administration from Webster University.

About the Contributor

Wes Weaver is the lead contributor of "TurnKey Investing with Lease-Options", a portfolio management book that teaches independent-minded investors how to *generate safe and steady returns* through real estate and the Turnkey Lease-Option Strategy.

With a state-approved work permit in hand at age 15, Wes had an early start in building character, maturity, and discipline, working for different businesses throughout his high school and college years. Working his way up, Wes became at age 21, one of the youngest commissioned salesperson in the food distribution industry.

Having achieved annual sales of over $1.3 million for his employer, Wes left the corporate world at the age of 24 to become a full-time real estate investor. Through his property management firm, Wes invests in real estate for himself and his investment partners. Today, Wes continues to enjoy the passive income generated by his real estate portfolio.

Seeking ongoing growth and education, Wes often travels and networks with entrepreneurs and investors outside of his area to bring fresh perspectives into his business. Through his contacts in the U.S., he continues to expand his knowledge base which he applies to his business.

The Management Team

Matthew Chan & Wes Weaver are the principals of Intrepid Capital Group, a privately-held management firm based in Columbus, Georgia.

Shortly after Matthew's move into Columbus, Matthew and Wes began a friendship that eventually led them to forge an alliance to buy, invest, and manage investment property together.

With focus and determination, Matthew and Wes have established themselves as the "#1 Source of Owner-Financed Homes" in the Greater Columbus, Georgia area. They specialize in selling single-family homes with "owner-financing" with their innovative TurnKey Lease-Options system.

Matthew and Wes have mastered the art and science of generating safe and steady returns through investment properties in their local area. The TurnKey Lease-Options System they implement is a customized Marketing & Management System they use to great strategic advantage.

Matthew and Wes take a deliberate tag-team approach to their management style. They often carry out a "divide and conquer" strategy but also come together when a "strength in numbers" style is required. Their unorthodox but effective management style allows them to create a management synergy that few individuals in their local area can match.

Backed by their support team and advisors, they are steadfast and decisive in their approach of buying, investing, and managing cash flow investment properties.

In these turbulent economic times, Matthew and Wes continue to be pillars of stability for their investment partners. The mantra they practice and implement is "Safe and steady returns through ongoing cash flow."

FREE AUDIO PROGRAM!

As a special bonus for reading this book, we invite you to download and listen to our audio commentary as supplemental material to this book.

It is our way of thanking you for making the commitment and to expand your investing horizons and exploring investment alternatives.

http://www.turnkeyinvesting.com/tkibonus

Recommended Resources

Books I Recommend to Expand Your Investment Mind:

"All About Escrow and Real Estate Closings" by Sandy Gadow
Brief: The mechanics of real estate closings in easy-to-read language

"Barron's Real Estate Handbook" by Jack Harris & Jack Friedman
Brief: Reference manual with real estate terms, definitions, & diagrams

"Every Landlord's Legal Guide" by M. Stewart, R. Warner, et al.
Brief: A good landlord guide and information resource on all 50 states

"Places Rated Almanac" by David Savageau
Brief: Excellent overview of over 300 U.S. city profiles & demographics

"Real Estate Quick and Easy" by Roy Maloney
Brief: Real estate concepts described with simple text and illustrations

"The 22 Immutable Laws of Marketing" by Al Ries & Jack Trout
Brief: The rules we follow when we market our business and properties

"The Intrepid Way" by Matthew S. Chan
Brief: Using the entrepreneurial lifestyle to create personal freedom

"The Intrepid Way II - Transformation" by Matthew S. Chan
Brief: Personal changes you must make to live the entrepreneurial lifestyle

Websites I Recommend:

Chamber of Commerce http://www.chamberofcommerce.com
Brief: Market research tool to locate Chambers of Commerce in the U.S.

Cornell University's Legal Information Institute
http://www.law.cornell.edu/topics/state_statutes3.html#property
Brief: State statutes on property law

HUD's Fair Housing Laws & Presidential Executive Orders
http://www.hud.gov/offices/fheo/FHLaws/index.cfm
Brief: Fair housing laws for property managers and landlords

U.S. Housing Market Analysis by the Meyers Group
http://www.housingusa.com
Brief: Housing market analysis overview of the U.S.

U.S. Census Bureau http://www.census.gov
Brief: Excellent market research tool provided by the U.S. government

PropertyBoss http://www.propertyboss.com
Brief: The property management software we use

QuickBooks http://www.quickbooks.com
Brief: The accounting software we use

TurnKey Investing http://www.turnkeyinvesting.com
Brief: The companion website to this book

OwnerFinanceHomes.com http://www.ownerfinancehomes.com
Brief: Our primary website for marketing our properties

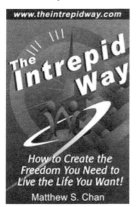

Ascend Beyond Publishing

www.ascendbeyond.com

Proof of Purchase

TurnKey Investing with Lease-Options Book